CALL for Background

STUDIES IN COMPUTER ASSISTED LANGUAGE LEARNING

Edited by Anna Turula

VOLUME 4

Prior to publication, the quality of the work published in this series is blind reviewed by an external referee appointed by the editor-ship. The referee is not aware of the author's name when performing the review.

Anna Turula / Anita Buczek-Zawiła (eds.)

CALL for Background

PETER LANG

Bibliographic Information published by the Deutsche Nationalbibliothek
The Deutsche Nationalbibliothek lists this publication in the Deutsche Nationalbibliografie; detailed bibliographic data is available in the internet at http://dnb.d-nb.de.

Library of Congress Cataloging-in-Publication Data
A CIP catalog record for this book has been applied for at the Library of Congress.

Cover illustration: Michał Kwaterski

This publication was financially supported by the Pedagogical University of Cracow.

ISSN 2364-1339
ISBN 978-3-631-84529-5 (Print)
E-ISBN 978-3-631-84919-4 (E-PDF)
E-ISBN 978-3-631-84920-0 (EPUB)
E-ISBN 978-3-631-84921-7 (MOBI)
DOI 10.3726/b18131

Peter Lang Edition is an Imprint of Peter Lang GmbH.

Peter Lang – Berlin · Bern · Bruxelles · New York · Oxford · Warszawa · Wien

This publication has been peer reviewed.

www.peterlang.com

Table of Contents

Anna Turula

Pedagogical University, Kraków, Poland

Anita Buczek-Zawiła

Pedagogical University, Kraków, Poland

Introduction

New technologies are a very useful educational tool. At the same time, they are just a tool, enabling the enhancement of pedagogy on condition that it is good pedagogy in the first place. This is why we call for CALL for background. What needs to be foregrounded are good educational practices, such as Content and Language Integrated Learning (CLIL), including the integration of coding into the language class; Project-Based Language Learning (PBLL); interest in the individual differences in language learning; language learning for special purposes and needs (LSP, LSN); focus on civic education, digital citizenship and 21st-century skills in the language class; internationalization of education; outdoor education and situated learning; arts and crafts in language learning; as well as broadly-understood innovation in the language classroom.

The themes listed above were the foci of the 2019 PL-CALL Conference held in Poland, at the Pedagogical University of Kraków. Many of the chapters included in this volume originated as papers delivered at this conference. Others were added in the process of compiling the volume. All address one issue, whose importance has grown with the COVID-19 pandemic, in which computer mediated education has become a standard; an issue which is expressed by the title of the volume and has already been stated above. It all starts and ends with good pedagogy. New technologies *always* come second; are always in the background.

Cédric Sarré introduces us to the combination of Information and Communication Technology (ICT) as adopted by teachers of Languages for Specific Purposes (LSP), so that LSP (and ESP in particular) can benefit from ICT affordances the special relationship between them offers. The Technology-mediated ESP Learning And Teaching (TESPLAT) arises as a result to be an emerging field of learning/teaching and research within pedagogy-driven ESP courses rather than technology-driven, favouring integrative course design.

Barbara Lewandowska-Tomaszczyk examines the linguistic resources by which two groups of students: Polish university students of English and American university non-language major express their judgment and arguments in online tasks, taking place in a virtual exchange (telecollaboration) within TAPP exchange. The analysis focuses on how the students discuss and argue their points of view in terms of their linguistic and cultural identities, reflections on their collaboration, surveys, and online interaction with regards to the essays and tasks they were performing during the period of collaboration.

In the chapter by **Anita Buczek-Zawiła**, a hybrid course on English phonetics and pronunciation (at English Studies Department, PUK), following a blended-course format and adhering to the metacomptence model of Wrembel (2005), is presented and evaluated. The objective is to demonstrate how new technologies of CAPT and the LMS of Moodle can enrich a fundamentally practical skill oriented-course, not losing sight of the primary objective of maximally eliminating accentedness on English.

Anna Ciechanowska via action research ventures to assess whether the level of linguistic skills and knowledge represented by undergraduate students is developed well enough to allow them to meet the demands of the translation market in the online economy and to determine what errors students make most frequently while performing translation tasks. That is followed by an attempt to account for the reasons behind these mistakes. The course of instruction itself is founded and developed on the assumption that it should reflect the real world working conditions, and hence the students are engaged in a business-like online environment where they provide translation services and where a translated text is a commodity that undergoes various stages for which the students remain accountable.

Natalia Góralczyk investigates English teachers' attitudes towards using new technologies in a foreign language classroom with older adults, demonstrating that though generally considered effective and beneficial, the selection needs to be geared towards preferences and specific needs of the learners. Some of these needs and preferences have stemmed from previous learning experiences or personal tastes in specific modes of learning, e.g. note-taking and presentations.

In the next chapter, **Lionel Nicolas, Julia Ostanina-Olszewska, Špela Arhar Holdt, Claudia Borg, Jaka Čibej, Verena Lyding,** and **Anabela Barreiro** discuss crowdsourcing opportunities for the language teaching community. More specifically, they elaborately present and argue for a crowdsourcing paradigm in which it is language learners themselves who produce exercise content via online tools. The authors also explore the potential of crowdsourcing to mass-produce content for a variety of exercises.

Robert Oliwa decides to determine if, and how, undergraduate English studies students are prepared to offer translation services in the changing online economy, all with the view to establishing what modifications to the existing study programmes should be introduced in order to cater for both students' and customers' needs through action research design. The conclusions prompt the author to suggest that augmenting the present programme of studies with the new content may develop the students' translation competence and, therefore, help them to stand out in job market.

eTwinning projects carried out in Polish schools and civic literacy are the subject of focus in the next chapter, written by **Anna Turula**. She looks at how civic literacy, as defined in Morgan (2016), can be effectively integrated into a virtual exchange (VE). It is argued here that eTwinning exchanges provide the most promising answer to the postulate of integrating civic literacy into the language classroom, especially when accompanied by raised teachers' awareness regarding the benefits of task design complexity as well as the fact that digital literacy goes way beyond the purely technical ICT expertise.

The last chapter by **Łukasz Zarzycki** explores YouTube's resources in order to clarify whether YouTube language learning video clips can play an educational role in language learning. The chapter offers a detailed analysis of different YouTube channels which are recommended for effective classroom application, together with the pedagogical assessment criteria aiding in their selection and class implementation.

We hope that each of the chapters provides for an interesting read. We believe that the authors have been successful in getting the message across: CALL for background.

Volume editors
Anna Turula & Anita Buczek-Zawiła

Cédric Sarré

Sorbonne Université – INSPE de Paris, CeLiSo (Centre de Linguistique en Sorbonne), Paris, France

Technology-Mediated ESP Learning And Teaching (TESPLAT): from language learning theory to ICT integration principles

Abstract: The slow adoption of Information and Communication Technology (ICT) by teachers of Languages for Specific Purposes (LSP), and of English for Specific Purposes (ESP) in particular is worth noting and can probably be attributed to the lack of specific training received by LSP teachers, but it is certainly not due to the fact that LSP/ESP cannot benefit from ICT affordances. It is therefore worth examining how ESP can precisely benefit from ICT affordances, the combination of ESP and ICT leading to Technology-mediated ESP Learning And Teaching (TESPLAT), an emerging field of learning/teaching and research. The benefits identified can indeed serve as the basis to determine a set of principles for successful ICT integration in ESP learning and teaching, which is one of the objectives of this contribution. To this end, the characteristics of ESP will first be discussed and the predominant language learning theory in ESP teaching will then be examined in relation to ESP objectives. The "special relationship" between ESP and ICT will then be studied and key principles to successful ICT integration in ESP learning and teaching will finally be outlined, the goal being to match ICT affordances to pedagogical considerations in an attempt to design pedagogy-driven ESP courses rather than technology-driven ones.

Keywords: ICT affordances, ICT integration, ESP, teacher education

1. Introduction

The way Information and Communication Technology (ICT) has been integrated into language teaching and learning has evolved considerably since the 1980s (Leffa 2009), moving from Higgins's 1988 conception of Computer-Assisted Language Learning (CALL) as a metaphor for the magister to Bax's 2003 concept of technology "normalization," that is to say a stage of technological integration that is such that technology almost goes unnoticed (for example, using a video projector/beamer in the classroom). Still, the literature consistently points to the slow adoption of ICT by language teachers, be it teachers of Languages for Specific Purposes (LSP) (Zourou & Torresin 2019), and, more specifically, of English for Specific Purposes (ESP) (Kumar & Rani 2016; Li 2018). If this can probably be attributed to the lack of specific training received by LSP teachers (Howard 1997; Master 1997; Basturkmen 2014; Braud et al. 2015; Brudermann et al. 2016), it is certainly not due to the fact that LSP/ESP cannot benefit from ICT affordances as several authors have noted to what extent LSP teaching can make the most of ICT integration (Delcloque 1997; Mamakou & Grigoriadou 2009; Belcher 2017; Li 2017; Muñoz-Luna & Taillefer 2018).

It is therefore worth examining how ESP can precisely benefit from ICT affordances, the combination of ESP and ICT leading to an emerging field of learning/teaching and research, that of Technology-mediated ESP Learning And Teaching (TESPLAT). To this end, the characteristics of ESP will first be discussed with special emphasis on the traditional – but outdated – dichotomy between ESP and what has been termed "General English (GE)." The predominant language learning theory in ESP teaching will then be examined as well as its methodological operationalization in relation to ESP objectives, before discussing the "special relationship" between ESP and ICT and outlining some key principles to successful ICT integration in ESP learning and teaching, the goal being to match ICT affordances to pedagogical considerations in an attempt to design pedagogy-driven ESP courses rather than technology-driven ones.

2. Characteristics of ESP

2.1. Defining characteristics of ESP

> ESP must be seen as an approach not as a product. ESP is not a particular type of language or methodology, nor does it consist of a particular type of teaching material. Understood properly, it is an approach to language learning, which is based on learner need. The foundation of all ESP is the simple question: Why does this learner need to learn a foreign language? (Hutchinson & Waters 1987: 19)

In their definition, Hutchinson & Waters (1987) clearly consider ESP as an approach to language learning, with strong emphasis on learner needs. A decade later, Dudley-Evans & St John (1998: 4–5) offered a more detailed definition which is comprised of absolute characteristics and variable characteristics and which does not really read like the definition of a construct but more like curricular guidelines aimed at ESP teachers. The focus therefore seems to be more on language teaching, this time. For example, the description of the language is only seen as a necessary step to the teaching of this particular type of language. From a French perspective, Petit's (2002) definition of ASP (*Anglais de Spécialité*) encapsulates the main differences with the formalization of ESP in the English speaking world. In the French school of ESP, the specialized varieties of the language are objects of study in their own right because they exist independently from what we would do with them in the classroom. These views are summarized in Table 1 below.

Table 1. A summary of ESP definitions (Sarré & Whyte 2016: 149).

HUTCHINSON & WATERS (1987)	DUDLEY-EVANS & ST JOHN (1998)	PETIT (2002)
ESP as an approach to language learning	ESP in terms of core characteristics and optional features of language teaching	ESP as a subdiscipline of English studies
Emphasis on learner needs	Emphasis on • learner needs • methodological choices in relation to professional contexts • linguistic aspects of specialized language	Emphasis on • the varied dimensions of specialized language: linguistic, discursive, cultural • the teaching of this subdiscipline

Building on Petit's (2002) definition, Sarré & Whyte (2016) put forward the following definition of ESP in the French context:

> The branch of English language studies which concerns the language, discourse and culture of English-language professional communities and specialised social groups, as well as the learning and teaching of this object from a didactic perspective (Sarré & Whyte 2016: 150).

As can be seen in this definition, ESP can be considered from two different perspectives which interact with each other: It is both "a research object aiming at characterizing the language, discourse and culture of specialized communities and a learning and teaching object" (Braud et al. 2015: 49). In that respect, the French perspective on ESP is worth mentioning as it seems to be more inclusive than previous formalizations of the concept in the English speaking world, covering both linguistic descriptions of specialized varieties of English (SVE) in the field of linguistics (from a discourse and genre analysis approach) and the learning and teaching of these specialized varieties of English in the fields of applied linguistics/didactics and language education.

In addition, following the example of Dudley-Evans & St John (1998), a number of variable and absolute characteristics of ESP learning and teaching were put forward by Sarré & Whyte (2016):

Absolute characteristics:

- Interaction between language and content knowledge: content and/or methodologies are derived from specific disciplines or occupations, the specialist domain (Douglas 2010);
- Goal-directedness: the objectives of ESP learning and teaching are specific and directed towards particular skills and knowledge (language and culture) of a given discipline or occupation, learner ability to complete tasks as "real-world activities";
- Needs analysis: the objectives of ESP learning and teaching are determined through careful needs analysis;
- Institutional constraints:
  - Student background and level: highly heterogeneous groups at university (slightly less so for more selective pathways – e.g. engineering schools)
  - ESP as a course requirement, which impacts student motivation
  - Group size
  - Contact time (very restricted)

Variable characteristics:

- Primacy of task completion (over language accuracy): performance vs. accuracy, ESP as an example of English as a *Lingua Franca* (ELF);
- Primacy of specific language skills development;
- Use of authentic materials;
- Use of specific methods: tasks (TBLT), project-based learning, CLIL;
- Use of language certification, specific ESP testing, development of ESP certification exams;
- Basic teacher training in ESP (often limited or absent) for non-research professionals.

(Sarré & Whyte 2016: 157)

2.2. Why teach ESP?

We can indeed wonder why we should teach ESP at all in Higher and Adult Education settings in particular. Besides the obvious need for the training offered in Higher Education to lead to successful integration in the world of work, which applies to language training as well (Braud et al. 2017), the first practical reason for teaching ESP is that learners in these settings often have a limited amount of time to learn the language: "As students in ESP classes often have restricted time to learn English, it makes sense to teach them only the bits of English they need" (Basturkmen 2006: 18). It is precisely because time is counted that ESP teachers need to be selective in what they want to teach: "As it is not possible to teach all of a language, teachers and course designers must be selective. Nowhere is this more so than in ESP teaching, with its emphasis on specific purposes and the limited duration of most ESP courses" (Basturkmen 2006: 23). In short, ESP teachers are faced with a sense of urgency and accuracy (Mangiante & Parpette 2004), which means that ESP teaching is usually geared towards "target language use situations" (Douglas 2001: 46).

2.3. Defining Specific Purpose Language Ability (SPLA)

Researchers in the field have noted the persisting discrepancies between the language skills developed and measured academically and the language skills most sought after by specialized communities (Zhang 2013; Hafner 2013). These discrepancies are also noticeable between the type of training offered to Higher Education students and the expectations of the industry (LEMP report 2015).

The specialized language skills needed by students is what has been termed Specific Purpose Language Ability (SPLA) (Douglas 2000). It is delineated by the common characteristics of different target language use situations and defined by recurrent genres and registers, and it is framed by the specialist domain of the learners' diploma/training. Finally, SPLA also draws from *English as a Lingua Franca* (ELF) as ESP is considered by some authors to be "the English as a *lingua franca* of the learning and working world" (Master 2005: 112). This means that ESP invites us "to rethink the established notions of competence" (Cogo & Dewey 2012: 167) and to accept that teaching native-like proficiency level is not what matters but rather effective communication in the language in a given situation.

Braud et al. (2017: 38) consider that SPLA is a micro-skill which is part of a professional macro-skill and which comprises three components: (1) a domain/profession-specific competence, that is to say the specialized skills expected from the academic/professional communities (culture, values, references, terminology, etc.), (2) the knowledge of specialized communication modes, that is to say the genres and registers specific to the specialist domain, (3) specialized social skills, that is to say the ability to interact within specialized discourse communities.

2.4. Two opposing perspectives: ESP vs General English?

Some authors (Bloor & Bloor 1986) consider ESP as a mere extension of a basic or common core of general language. This notion of common core (Corder 1993) has been defined as "a general pool of language of high frequency items that predominates all uses of languages" (Basturkmen 2006: 16). In other words, this means that different varieties of a language are based on common linguistic features (grammar, lexis, etc.) which make up the common core of general language. Pedagogically speaking, this view of language implies that it is necessary for learners to master the common core of English before introducing ESP (Quirk et al. 1972; Coxhead & Nation 2001). And then only "when learners have mastered control of the 2,000 words of general usefulness in English, it is wise to direct vocabulary learning to more specialized areas depending on the aims of the learners" (Coxhead & Nation 2001: 252–253). This perspective therefore seems to offer a very limited view of LSPs as the main focus is terminology (i.e. specialized vocabulary). This view is implicitly adhered to by the authors of the CEFR if we closely examine the descriptors of proficiency levels on the global scale (Table 2).

Table 2. Common reference levels: Global scale from the CEFR (Council of Europe 2001: 24).

PROFICIENT USER	C2	Can understand with ease virtually everything heard or read. Can summarise information from different spoken and written sources, reconstructing arguments and accounts in a coherent presentation. Can express him/herself spontaneously, very fluently and precisely, differentiating finer shades of meaning even in more complex situations.
	C1	Can understand a wide range of demanding, longer texts, and recognise implicit meaning. Can express him/herself fluently and spontaneously without much obvious searching for expressions. Can use language flexibly and effectively for social, academic and professional purposes. Can produce clear, well-structured, detailed text on complex subjects, showing controlled use of organisational patterns, connectors and cohesive devices.
INDEPENDENT USER	B2	Can understand the main ideas of complex text on both concrete and abstract topics, including technical discussions in his/her field of specialisation. Can interact with a degree of fluency and spontaneity that makes regular interaction with native speakers quite possible without strain for either party. Can produce clear, detailed text on a wide range of subjects and explain a viewpoint on a topical issue giving the advantages and disadvantages of various options.
	B1	Can understand the main points of clear standard input on familiar matters regularly encountered in work, school, leisure, etc. Can deal with most situations likely to arise whilst travelling in an area where the language is spoken. Can produce simple connected text on topics which are familiar or of personal interest. Can describe experiences and events, dreams, hopes & ambitions and briefly give reasons and explanations for opinions and plans.

We can see that, if level B1 makes no reference to specialized contexts, discourses or language, level B2 mentions the ability to take part in "technical discussions in his/her **field of specialization**," and, further up on the scale, level C1 mentions the ability to "use language flexibly and effectively for social, **academic** and **professional purposes**" (my emphasis). It is quite clear that, in this view, specialization (in the form of language for academic and professional purposes) means complexity, since a learner's proficiency level has to be higher to be able to deal with these specialized varieties of the language. Does this mean that (1) no specialization is possible below level B1 or that (2) all academic and professional contexts require language learners to have a command of the language equivalent to level C1 for effective communication to be possible?

The second perspective on ESP contends the very opposite: in this view, there is no common core of language pre-existing to varieties; basic language is what is common to all varieties of English, and these varieties overlap (Bloor & Bloor 1986). Some authors take this argument one step further and claim that there is no "general purpose" language, no General English, which means that all language is specific purpose. In other words, and quite provocatively, there is no "English for no purpose" (Douglas 2010: 9). From a pedagogical point of view, languages are always learnt in a specific context:

> All language learning is acquired from one variety or another, even if it's "classroom English" variety. The language learner is as likely to acquire "the language" from one variety as from another, but the use of language, being geared to situation and participants, is learned in appropriate contexts (Bloor & Bloor 1986: 28).

In this respect, it is also interesting to note that the assumption that it is necessary to acquire a "common core" of the language before introducing language for specific purposes (LSP) is not supported by research (Hyland 2002: 388). In addition, the argument which links specialization of a language with its complexity is unfounded: for example, Mangiante (2017) showed that there is no correlation between specialization and complexity in the case of French for Specific Purposes, as specialized discourses made accessible to the general public are often more syntactically complex than the original (more specialized) discourses. In other words, this means that it is possible to teach and learn a specific variety of a language at any proficiency level and that there is no need to wait for learners to reach a certain proficiency level (B2, for example) to introduce ESP.

2.5. Towards a continuum of specificity

Today, the debate between the proponents of these opposing views seems somewhat outdated if we look at the evolving national curricula for languages in secondary education in different countries: for example, the latest revisions of the national curriculum in France[1] have introduced more possibilities than ever to teach the specialized varieties of a language through the promotion of Content and Language Integrated Learning (CLIL) at all levels of the education system… and these learners are definitely not all C1 students. As a result, it seems wiser and more in tune with today's changing world to consider language

1 For details see: https://eduscol.education.fr/cid46517/sections-europeennes-langues-orientales-selo.html.

on a "continuum of specificity" (Douglas 2010: 10) or continuum of specialization, which would span from "English conversation," to "Medical English" and to "English for Cardiac Nursing" in the case of ESP (Figure 1).

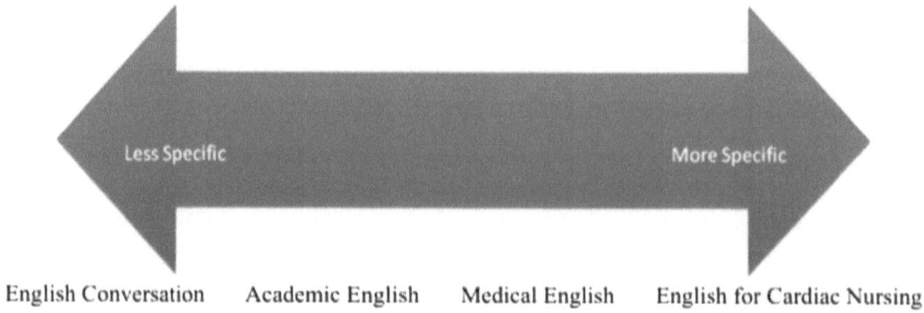

Figure 1. A continuum of Specificity (Douglas 2010: 10).

In this way, it also becomes possible to identify different grains of specificity within a given language, the continuum spanning from coarser grains to finer grains of specificity (Figure 2). As can be seen, specificity is determined not only by the type of language needed in a given context but also by the familiarity of the learner with the context of use (hence why English for General Professional Purposes can be considered to be more specific than English for Specific Academic Purposes, for example).

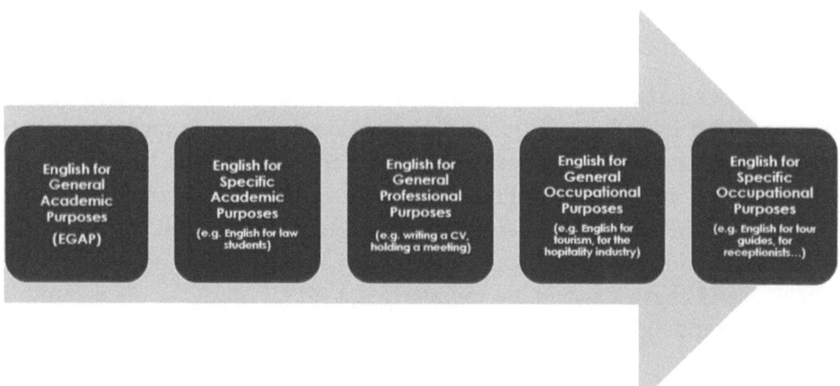

Figure 2. Different grains of specificity within ESP (Sarré 2018).

In Tertiary Education, the ESP curriculum could therefore make the most of these different grains, with each level of education being based on one (or more) of these in accordance with the degree of specialization that is required at each level of study. Figure 3 gives the example of the ESP curriculum in the French Higher Education system where course specialization is very progressive in the first three years of tertiary education (Bachelor's level) and then becomes more effective in years 4 and 5 (Master's level), and totally built in at Doctoral level.

The next question is to know what language learning theory predominates in ESP teaching and what methodology to use.

3. Teaching ESP: language learning/teaching theory and methodology

3.1. Socio-constructivist ESP

When it comes to teaching ESP, socio-constructivism is claimed to be the most relevant language learning theory as it mirrors academic and professional contexts which often imply collaboration:

> [T]he interpretation and construction of knowledge must be dependent on the cultural and social collaborative context. This is absolutely appropriate for adult learners that need to develop academic and professional/vocational discipline-specific language skills through a collaborative setting. Socioconstructivism, therefore, proves to be the appropriate paradigm for ESP learning in tertiary education (Mamakou & Grigoriadou 2009: 463).

This more recent (and current) socio-constructivist view of ESP considers the language learner's experience as an active social process aiming at constructing knowledge through social interaction (Vygotsky 1978). The variety of language learning theories obviously impacts language teaching which can be viewed as "an integrative design process model that integrates the learning modalities dictated by various learning theories" (Mamakou & Grigoriadou 2009: 460). The most appropriate operationalization of the socio-constructivist paradigm is Task-Based Language Teaching (TBLT).

3.2. ESP and TBLT

ESP's status as an international language or a *Lingua Franca* in the industry has helped us redefine what *being competent in ESP* means through our definition of Specific Purpose Language Ability (SPLA) (in section 2.3.): our "conceptualization of expertise, or proficient specialist language use" (Belcher 2006: 150) is therefore redefined thanks to a "shift in focus away from

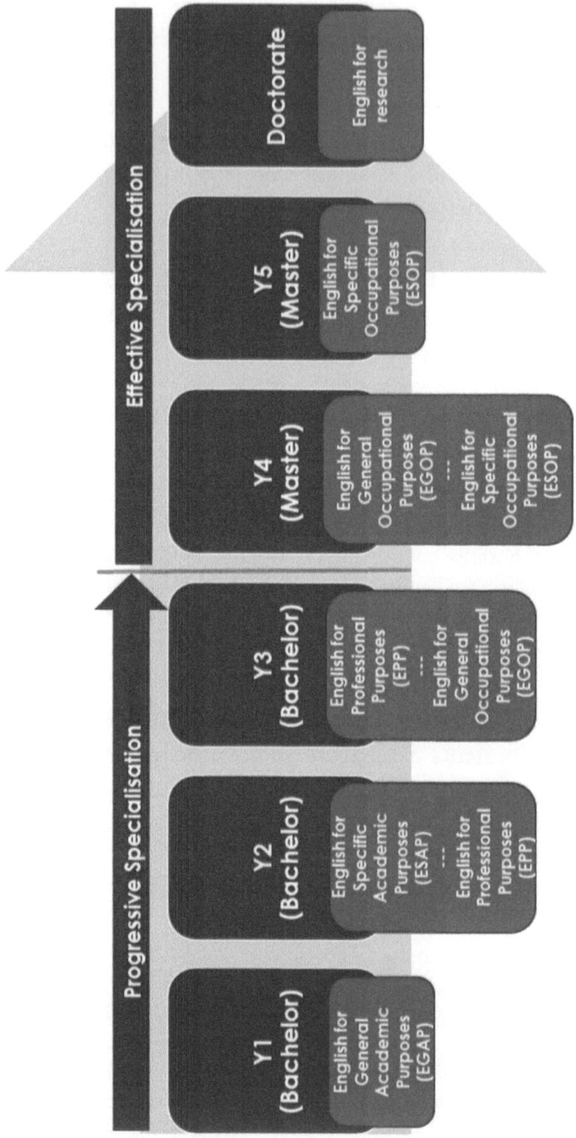

Figure 3. Different grains of specificity in the Higher Education ESP Curriculum (Sarré 2018).

proficiency to strategic communication" (Nickerson 2005: 369), that is to say through the development of communicatively effective strategies regardless of the ESP learner's proficiency level in the language. In other words, we have come to realize that "native speaker norms are not the most relevant in LSP" precisely because "formal linguistic accuracy is of little importance in any real-world context outside the language classroom" (Whyte 2019: 17). This is of particular importance to ESP teaching: it is therefore no wonder that its operational realization has taken the form of tasks, i.e. pedagogical tools which are at the core of Task-Based Language Teaching (TBLT) and which are "centrally concerned with the learner achieving some purpose and outcome, and do not directly require the use of conformity-oriented language" (Skehan 2001: 167). The characteristics of tasks can be defined through the following three quotes:

1. Tasks are defined as pieces of work in everyday life with a specific objective, such as painting a fence, filling in a form, making an airline reservation. They are non-linguistic units. (Basturkmen 2006 : 92)
2. An activity which requires learners to use language, with emphasis on meaning, to attain an objective. (Bygate, Skehan & Swain 2001: 11)
3. A workplan that requires learners to process language pragmatically in order to achieve an outcome that can be evaluated in terms of whether the correct or appropriate propositional content has been conveyed. (Ellis 2003: 17)

As a result, TBLT is specific about what learners need to communicate about and what actions they need to complete but not about what structures or vocabulary they need to use (Ellis 1998). If the acquisitional potential of tasks lies in the negotiation of meaning episodes that arise during task completion (cf. Interaction Hypothesis, Long 1983, 1996), it has been shown that tasks on their own are not as efficient as a "task + micro-tasks" sequence (i.e. post-task activities or pedagogical tasks) in order to help learners notice the gap in their knowledge/abilities (Robinson et al. 2001). Generally speaking, it is possible to claim that ESP has strong natural affinities with tasks since ESP teaching often makes the most of the "deep-end strategy" (Dudley-Evans & St John 1998: 190): learners are first put in a situation where they need to use the language to communicate and perform some activity and afterwards it is possible to focus on the aspects of the language that were problematic for them; their performance while completing a task is therefore the starting point, followed by post-task activities meant to help them notice the gap in their knowledge and abilities. The question is now to know how Information and Communication Technology (ICT) can support ESP teaching.

4. ESP and ICT: from ICT Affordances to ICT Integration Principles

4.1. ESP and ICT: a "special relationship"

First, it is interesting to note that ESP and ICT seem to have a number of specific affinities, a phenomenon we could call a "special relationship." Indeed, if we first focus on the most common ESP teaching and learning contexts, it has been shown that Higher Education and Adult Education settings offer teachers more freedom, that is to say more opportunities to experiment (with different ICT tools, for example) than other educational contexts as ESP teaching is sometimes qualified as "innovative" (Mémet & Petit 2001: 8; Hyland 2006: 35). Besides, in terms of specific constraints attached to ESP learning and teaching, large class size and the varying degrees of learner motivation (Sarré & Whyte 2016) call for a more pressing need for online or blended classes, which is one example of ICT integration. In addition, the typical ESP learner often has a more advanced proficiency level and is more autonomous (cf. the Higher Education and Adult Education settings), which means they are more able to cope with fewer face-to-face (F2F) sessions and can be offered more online/blended learning opportunities. When it comes to course objectives, ESP teaching can make the most of tools and environments that make it possible to recreate and simulate real-life work and academic environments and tasks. Finally, in terms of course content, using ICT in ESP teaching means it will be more in tune with the learners' specialist domains for those involved in computer science.

4.2. ICT affordances for ESP Teaching

Put simply, ICT affordances can be defined as the "potential benefits that technology can bring to the process of teaching and learning" (Li 2018: 10). Generally speaking, it has been shown that ICT can support language learning in many different ways: it fosters lexical acquisition, improves writing, listening comprehension and grammar accuracy (Macaro et al. 2012, review article). More specifically, Computer-Mediated Communication (CMC) also helps develop communication skills, intercultural awareness and collaboration skills (Macaro et al. 2012). The question is to know whether ICT has specific affordances for ESP teaching and learning.

In their review paper of 55 studies on the use of ICT in ESP teaching, Dashtestani & Stojkovic (2016) have shown that ICT use in ESP is different to that in EFL (English as a Foreign Language) teaching: more interest seems to be shown in the use of CMS/LMS for online learning, corpora and wikis. In

Table 3. Affordances of ICT linked to ESP learner needs (Li 2017: 142).

WHAT LEARNERS NEED	HOW TECHNOLOGY CAN HELP (EXAMPLES)
Communication skills	CMC tools (e.g., online discussion boards, emails and videoconferencing) can be used to engage students in real-life discourse
Academic writing skills	Corpus analysis of published academic work to identify how to use linking words, reporting verbs and tenses
Collaborative experience	Wikis, project-based CALL
Engagement and participation in a professional community	The use of social networking

addition, they were able to report the positive impact on ESP learning of these three technologies: (1) CMS/LMS (Course/Learning management Systems) tend to increase the quality of ESP instruction and to promote the development of listening skills; (2) corpora (large collections of texts in electronic format combined with specific tools such as concordancers) increase ESP students' knowledge of specialized vocabulary and collocations and foster academic communicative skills; (3) wikis enhance ESP students' knowledge of academic writing through collaborative writing activities. Still, these authors also note the persistent lack of empirical studies on the impact of other technologies on ESP learning (blogs, chat, discussion boards, IWBs, virtual worlds, social networking…) (Dashtestani & Stojkovic 2016).

Li (2018: 11–13) also outlines a number of potential affordances of ICT to ESP teaching and learning: in addition to the fact that ICT can support language learning by addressing learner needs (Table 3 below), it also facilitates the creation of authentic materials (digital web materials in particular), mediates thinking (in network-based learning and computer supported collaborative learning), provides a learning environment that makes interaction possible, facilitates self-directed learning (ICT offers learner the degree of control they need for self-direction), and motivates and engages learners.

4.3. ICT Integration Principles

It is of utmost importance to make sure that ICT is *integrated* in ESP teachers' practice and not simply *used,* which calls for a set of integration principles. In other words, ICT integration principles are necessary to ensure that ESP courses are pedagogy-driven as opposed to technology-driven. Following in the footsteps of Li (2018), we have identified a set of four integration principles:

P1 – Adopting a reflective approach to ICT integration

The critical analysis of ICT integration is essential to ensure that ICT is not a simple add-on and that its added value is real. In other words, the ESP teacher should question their use of ICT by trying to answer the following question: with the introduction of technology in task development "what can I do differently that I couldn't do before?" (Holtzman 2009: 537). Does integrating ICT mean doing the same things as before but differently or does it mean doing other things that I could not necessarily do before? The answer to this question will reveal the real value added of technology.

The "integration" of ICT can sometimes be detrimental to the type of pedagogical approach the teacher would like to adopt: the focus can indeed be too much on technology and not enough on pedagogy. In order to help ESP teacher analyse their integration of technology, a number of critical models can be used. Two such models are presented below: Puentedura's (2010) SAMR model and the RAT model (Hughes 2005) (Figure 4). The idea of these models is to help teachers assess the extent to which ICT has been integrated by providing three (RAT) or four (SAMR) degrees of integration associated with specific descriptors.

Both models invite the teacher to reflect upon the role of technology in a given task: does it work as a substitute of existing tools commonly used in ESP teaching, with or without augmentation (enhancement level), or does it allow for a significant redesign of tasks (transformation level)? Obviously, the closer to transformation the role of technology is, the more value added it offers.

P2. Embracing the evolution of the ESP teachers' role

ICT integration often leads to a redefinition of the ESP teacher's role, as shown by Li (2018) (Table 4). Each of the roles outlined below calls for the use of one specific tool/technology. However hard it may be to accept change for teachers, as is also the case in any human organization or social group, ESP teachers should accept that their main role is to support language learning and not necessarily control it.

P3. Making the most of ICT affordances to promote authenticity (language, task)

Promoting authenticity of the language and tasks in ESP can be achieved by (1) accessing authentic materials online to use as teaching materials, (2) using corpora of field-specific texts to uncover authentic patterns of language use,

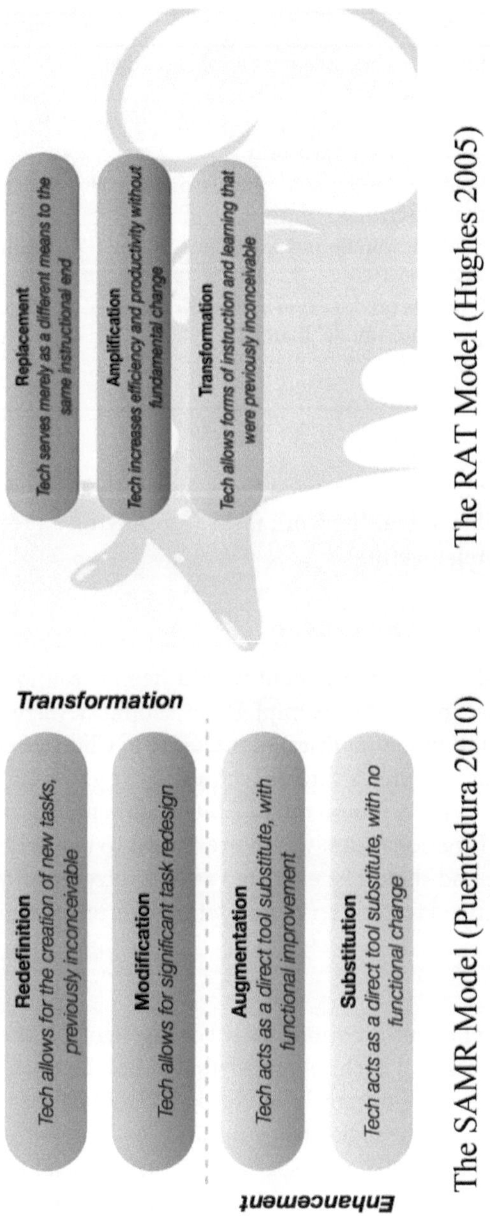

Figure 4. Two Critical Models for ICT Integration Analysis.

Table 4. The evolving Teacher's roles (Li 2018: 16).

TEACHER ROLE	ACTIVITY	TECHNOLOGY
Organizer	Students work together on collaborative writing projects	Wikis
Audience/reader	Students present their views and opinions about topics in their field	Blogs
Guide	Students develop a vocabulary project for their discipline	Corpus
Participant/ facilitator	Students initiate and participate in discussion	Online forum
Evaluator	Students produce oral and written work (with multimodal material)	Digital recording software and Microsoft Office package

(3) using ICT environments to provide tasks and communication modes that are as close as possible to real-life work tasks (e.g. solving a problem as a team in a videoconferencing meeting).

P4. Being innovative and daring

ESP teachers should dare to experiment with different technologies and tools (teaching with social media, for example) and should never wait to master a tool's full potential (all functionalities) to integrate it. Chances are that the first few attempts at using a complex tool or technology (e.g. the Interactive White Board) are going to be rather low on the ICT integration models presented above simply because the functionalities, which are easiest to use, will be tried out at first. This is normal and should be expected as ICT integration is a progressive endeavour closely linked to the user's confidence with using a given tool.

5. Conclusion

To conclude, this contribution aimed at shedding light on the clear parallel between two components of Technology-Mediated ESP Learning and Teaching (TESPLAT): (1) the predominantly socio-constructivist paradigm of ESP teaching to promote active social learning and, consequently, the pedagogical approaches adopted in ESP classes (action-based, social tasks, real-world activities) and (2) the evolution of ICT tools and the Internet, from informative resources (tutor) to tools to communicate (collaborative/interactive environments). Indeed, both elements seem to converge towards more social practice, which highlights their high complementarity. This also means that ICT's affordances for ESP learning and teaching are real, but so is the need for ICT integration principles to ensure that the ESP courses designed are pedagogy-driven and not technology-driven.

However, and in spite of the convergence mentioned above, there is still a number of difficulties and concerns in ICT integration into language teaching, especially among ESP teachers (Li 2018). This can probably be attributed to ESP teachers' lack of awareness, more comfort with text environments, sometimes deficient computer literacy, and their contentedness that technology does not deliver educational success (Virkus 2008). As a consequence, ESP teacher education in ICT integration seems more necessary than ever, which explains why it is at the heart of some recent European projects (cf. the CATAPULT Project[2]) which will contribute to the provision of adequate LSP teacher continuing professional development courses.

Finally, a research agenda specific to TESPLAT should be set out as "research on technology and ESP instruction seems to be in its infancy" (Dashtestani & Stojkovic 2016: 451). Indeed, more empirical research is still needed today to investigate the efficacy of certain technologies in ESP learning and teaching: text chat and blogs, Interactive White Boards, e-portfolios, automatic speech recognition, to name but a few technologies whose impact on ESP learning and teaching still needs investigating. Besides, it has been noted that more quantitative and experimental studies are needed in TESPLAT as the majority of studies to date in the field are qualitative in nature. TESPLAT's research agenda therefore seems wide open.

References

Basturkmen, H. (2014). LSP teacher education: Review of literature and suggestions for the research agenda. *Iberica*, *28*, 17–34.

Basturkmen, H. (2006). *Ideas and Options in English for Specific Purposes*. Mahwah, New Jersey: Lawrence Erlbaum.

Bax, S. (2003). CALL – past, present and future. *System*, *31*(1), 13–28.

Belcher, D. D. (2017). Recent Developments in ESP Theory and Research: Enhancing Critical Reflection and Learner Autonomy through Technology and Other Means. In: Stojković, N., Tošić, M. & V. Nejković

2 The project website http://www.catapult-project.eu.

(Eds.), *Synergies of English for Specific Purposes and Language Learning Technologies* (pp. 2–19). Newcastle upon Tyne: Cambridge Scholars Publishing.

Belcher, D. D. (2006). English for specific purposes: Teaching to perceived needs and imagined futures in worlds of work, study, and everyday life. *TESOL quarterly*, *40*(1), 133–156.

Bloor, M., & Bloor, T. (1986). Languages for Specific Purposes: Practice and Theory. *Occasional Paper-Centre for Language and Communication Studies*, *19*, 1–35.

Blue, G. (1988). Individualising academic writing tuition. In P. C. Robinson (Ed.), *Academic writing: Process and product* (ELT Documents 129) (pp. 95–99). London: Modern English Publications.

Braud, V., Millot, P., Sarré, C., & Wozniak, S. (2017). Quelles conceptions de la maîtrise de l'anglais en contexte professionnel? Vers une définition de la compétence en anglais de spécialité, *Mélanges CRAPEL*, *n°37*, 13–44.

Braud, V., Millot, P., Sarré, C., & Wozniak, S. (2015). Pour une formation de tous les anglicistes à la langue de spécialité. *Les Langues Modernes*, *n°3/* 2015, 67–76.

Brudermann, C., Mattioli, M. A., Roussel, A. M., & Sarré, C. (2016). Le secteur des langues pour spécialistes d'autres disciplines dans les universités françaises: résultats d'une enquête nationale menée par la SAES. *Recherche et pratiques pédagogiques en langues de spécialité. Cahiers de l'Apliut*, *35* (numéro spécial).

Bruner, J. S. (1978). The role of dialogue in language acquisition. In A. Sinclair, R. Jarvella & W. J. M. Levelt (Eds.), *The child's conception of language* (pp. 241–256). New York: Springer-Verlag.

Bygate, M., Skehan, P., & Swain, M. (2001). *Researching pedagogic tasks: -Second language learning, teaching, and testing*. London: Longman.

Cogo, A., & Dewey, M. (2012). *Analysing English as a lingua franca: A corpus-driven investigation*. London: Continuum.

Corder, S. P. (1993). *Introducing applied linguistics*. London: Penguin.

Council of Europe. (2001). *Common European framework of reference for languages: Learning, teaching, assessment*. Cambridge: Cambridge University Press.

Coxhead, A., & Nation, P. (2001). The specialised vocabulary of English for academic purposes. In: Flowerdew, J. & M. Peacock (Eds.), *Research perspectives on English for academic purposes* (pp. 252–267). Cambridge: Cambridge University Press.

Dashtestani, R. & Stojkovic, N. (2016). The use of technology in English for Specific Purposes (ESP) instruction: A literature review. *Journal of Teaching English for Specific and Academic Purposes, 3*(3), 435–456.

Delcloque, P. (1997). LSP teacher training in the use of technology: Overcoming technofear. In R. Howard & G. Brown (Eds.), *Teacher education for Languages for Specific Purposes* (pp. 103–113). Clevedon: Multilingual Matters.

Douglas, D. (2010). This Won't hurt a bit: Assessing English for Nursing. *Taiwan International ESP Journal, 2*(2), 1–16.

Douglas, D. (2001). Three problems in testing language for specific purposes: Authenticity, specificity and inseparability. In C. Elder, A. Brown, E. Grove, K. Hill, N. Iwashita, T. Lumley, T. McNamara & K. O'Loughlin (Eds.), *Experimenting with uncertainty: Essays in honour of Alan Davies* (pp. 45–52). Cambridge: Cambridge University Press.

Douglas, D. (2000). *Assessing Languages for Specific Purposes.* Cambridge: Cambridge University Press.

Dudley-Evans, T., & St John, M. J. (1998). *Developments in English for Specific Purposes: A multi-disciplinary approach.* Cambridge: Cambridge University Press.

Ellis, R. (2003). *Task-based language learning and teaching.* Oxford: Oxford University Press.

Ellis, R. (1998). The evaluation of communicative tasks. In B. Tomlinson (Ed.), *Materials development in language teaching* (pp. 217–238). Cambridge: Cambridge University Press.

Hafner, C. A. (2013). The discursive construction of professional expertise: Appeals to authority in barrister's opinion. *English for Specific Purposes, 32*(3), 131–143.

Higgins, J. (1988). *Language, learners, and computers: Human intelligence and artificial unintelligence.* London: Longman.

Hughes, J. (2005). The Role of Teacher Knowledge and Learning Experiences in Forming Technology-integrated Pedagogy. *Journal of Technology and Teacher Education, 13*(2), 277–302.

Holtzman, S. (2009). Web 2.0 and CMS for second language learning. In M. Thomas (Ed.), *Handbook of research on web 2.0 and second language learning* (pp. 526–545). Hershey, PA: IGI Global.

Howard, R. (1997). LSP in the UK. In R. Howard, & G. Brown (Eds.), *Teacher education for Languages for Specific Purposes* (pp. 41–57). Clevedon: Multilingual Matters.

Hutchinson, T. & Waters, A. (1987). *English for Specific Purposes.* Cambridge: Cambridge University Press.

Hyland, K. (2006). The "other" English: Thoughts on EAP and academic writing. *The European English Messenger 15/2*, 34–38.

Hyland, K. (2002). Specificity revisited: How far should we go? *English for Specific Purposes, 21*(4), 385–395.

Kumar, S., & Rani, M. (2016). Attitudes of teachers towards the use of technology and innovation in the classroom. *International Journal of Research in IT and Management, 6*(11), 26–34.

Leffa, V. J. (2009). CALL as action. In R. de Cássia Veiga Marriott & P. Lupion Torres (Eds.), *Handbook of research on e-learning methodologies for language acquisition* (pp. 39–52). Hershey, NY: IGI Global.

LEMP (2015). *Languages and employability: Analysis of the foreign language skills requirements of French employers.* LEMP Consortium, retrieved from < https://www.ciep.fr/expertise-audit-langues/langues-etrangeres-et-mobilite/langues-employabilite>

Li, L. (2018). Integrating Technology in ESP: Pedagogical Principles and Practice. In R. Muñoz-Luna & L. Taillefer (Eds.), *Integrating Information and Communication Technologies in English for Specific Purposes* (pp. 7–25). Cham, Switzerland: Springer.

Li, L. (2017). *New technologies and language learning.* London: Palgrave Macmillan.

Long, M. H. (1996). The role of the linguistic environment in second language acquisition. In W. Ritchie & T. Bhatia (Eds.), *Handbook of second language acquisition* (pp. 413–468). San Diego: Academic Press Inc.

Long, M. H. (1983). Native speaker/non-native speaker conversation and the negotiation of comprehensible input. *Applied Linguistics, 4*, 126–141.

Macaro, E., Handley, Z., & Walter, C. (2012). A systematic review of CALL in English as a second language: Focus on primary and secondary education. *Language Teaching, 45*(1), 1–43.

Mamakou, I. & Grigoriadou, M. (2009). Project-based instruction for ESP in Higher Education. In R. de Cássia Veiga Marriott & P. Lupion Torres (Eds.), *Handbook of research on e-learning methodologies for language acquisition* (pp. 456–479). Hershey, NY: IGI Global.

Mangiante, J.-M. (2017). Le cas du FOS: quels descripteurs pour le français sur objectifs spécifiques? One-day conference "Langue de spécialité: spécialization, diversité et langue générale," Université Lille 3, 16 juin 2017.

Mangiante, J.-M. & Parpette, C. (2004). *Le français sur objectif spécifique: de l'analyse des besoins à l'élaboration d'un cours.* Paris: Hachette.

Master, P. (2005). Research in English for specific purposes. In E. Hinkel (Ed.), *Handbook of research in second language teaching and learning* (pp. 99–116). London/New York: Routledge.

Master, P. (1997). ESP teacher education in the USA. In R. Howard & G. Brown (Eds.), *Teacher education for Languages for Specific Purposes* (pp.22–40). Clevedon: Multilingual Matters.

Mémet, M. & Petit, M. (Eds.). (2001). *L'anglais de spécialité en France: Mélanges en l'honneur de Michel Perrin*. Bordeaux: GERAS Éditeur.

Muñoz-Luna, R. & Taillefer, L. (Eds.). (2018). *Integrating Information and Communication Technologies in English for Specific Purposes*. New York: Springer International Publishing.

Nickerson, C. (2005). English as a lingua franca in international business contexts. *English for Specific Purposes, 24*(4), 367–380.

Petit, M. (2002). "Éditorial." *ASp, 35/36*, 1–3.

Puentedura, R. (2010). SAMR and TPCK – Intro to Advanced Practice. Retrieved from < http://hippasus.com/resources/sweden2010/SAMR_TPCK_IntroToAdvancedPractice.pdf>

Quirk, R., Greenbaum, S., Leech, G., & Svartik, J. (1972). *A grammar of contemporary English*. London: Longman.

Robinson, P., Strong, G., Whittle, J., & Nobe, S. (2001). The development of EAP oral discussion ability. In J. Flowerdew & M. Peacock (Eds.), *Research perspectives on English for Academic Purposes* (pp. 347–360). Cambridge: Cambridge University Press.

Sarré, C. (2018). Enseigner les langues en secteur LANSAD: pourquoi et comment les langues de spécialité s'imposent-elles comme «objets naturels» d'enseignement-apprentissage et avec quelles conséquences? "Enseignement-apprentissage de langue de spécialité, professionnelle ou générale: Quels besoins, objectifs, approches et supports?" Conference, Université Paris 1 Panthéon-Sorbonne, 13 December 2018.

Sarré, C. & Whyte, S. (2016). Research in ESP teaching and learning in French higher education: developing the construct of ESP didactics, *ASp, 69*, 139–164.

Skehan, P. (2001). Tasks and language performance. In M. Bygate, P. Skehan, and M. Swain (Eds.), *Researching pedagogic tasks: Second language learning, teaching, and testing* (pp. 167–185). London: Longman.

Virkus, S. (2008). Use of Web 2.0 technologies in LIS education: Experiences at Tallin University, Estonia. In L. Tedd (Ed.), *Program: Electronic library and information systems* (pp. 262–274). Bingley: Emerald.

Vygotsky, L. S. (1978). *Mind in society: The development of higher psychological processes.* Cambridge, MA: Harvard University Press.

Whyte, S. (2019). Revisiting Communicative Competence in the Teaching and Assessment of Language for Specific Purposes. *Language Education & Assessment*, 2(1),1–19.

Zhang, Z. (2013). Business English students learning to write for international business: What do international business practitioners have to say about their texts? *English for Specific Purposes*, *32*(3), 144–156.

Zourou, K., & Torresin, G. (2019). *CATAPULT Situational Survey: LSP teachers' needs for skills and training.* CATAPULT Consortium. Retrieved from < http://catapult-project.eu/?smd_process_download=1&download_id=1030 >

Online sources

https://eduscol.education.fr/cid46517/sections-europeennes-langues-orientales-selo.html

http://www.catapult-project.eu

Barbara Lewandowska-Tomaszczyk

State University of Applied Sciences in Konin, Poland

Judgment and argumentation in cross-cultural online collaboration between native and non-native students

Abstract: The present study examines the linguistic resources by which two groups of students: Polish university students of English and American university non-language major express their judgment and arguments in online tasks, taking place in a virtual exchange (telecollaboration) within TAPP exchange during four semesters of their studies (2017/2019). More specifically, the study attempts to analyse how the students discuss and argue their points of view in terms of their linguistic and cultural identities with reference to the issue under discussion. Data triangulation includes reflections on their collaboration, surveys, and online interaction with regards to the essays and tasks they were performing during the period of collaboration.

Keywords: argumentation, judgment, native students, non-native students, online collaboration (telecollaboration), TAPP

1. Introduction: Language, judgment, and argument

The ways in which judgments are expressed in language or behaviour make the content persuasive and rely, as proposed by Martin Hinton (2019), with regard to Gilbert (2004: 260–261), on the *convince/persuade* dichotomy. Hinton proposes that "*persuasion* and its handmaiden – *emotion* – are bad, and *convincing* with its valet, *reason*, are good." (italics mine), as persuasion is not considered to be based on reasoned arguments. However, the author argues further, such a distinction is difficult to maintain as any argument expressed in language cannot be separated from considerations of persuasive rhetorical impact. The present study brings to light and exemplifies some differences in judgment and argumentative structure – combined with their rhetorical value – Polish and American students employ in their interactive task correspondence with their pairs and in their peer corrective feedback. At the same time, both the US as well as Polish students are exposed to the other culture in their collaborative tasks, which creates a conductive context for them to develop aspects of their (pluri-) linguistic and (pluri-) cultural identities, discussed in the study.

2. Research objectives

The present study focuses on the expression of judgment and argumentation in online tasks, taking place in a virtual exchange (telecollaboration) within the TAPP collaborative online tasks between American native students of non-language courses at the University of Minnesota and Polish MA philology (language) students of the State University of Applied Sciences in Konin. A more specific analysis of the data is targeted towards linguistic and discursive similarities and differences between the two groups in terms of their distinct language competences, and linguistic and cultural identities, particularly with respect to the nature of the justification and argumentative strategies used by Polish and American students in their intercultural interaction.

3. Trans-Atlantic & Pacific Project (TAPP)

The Trans-Atlantic & Pacific Project (TAPP), which links students in different countries in collaborative teams, was launched in 1999/2000 by North Dakota State University represented by Bruce Maylath and Sonia Vandepitte of Ghent University in Belgium. The TAPP network has developed a number of different categories of native – non-native student collaboration (e.g., Maylath et al. 2013) and promotes development of language and language-based skills in terms of *doing by writing* with particular emphasis on (inter-)cultural awareness raising and practice.

3.1. Collaborative procedure

The TAPP collaborative projects involving American students and students of the State University of Applied Sciences in Konin have been conducted for over four years now. The first two years were coordinated by Heather Slomski of the North Dakota State University and Concordia College and the author of the present paper (Lewandowska-Tomaszczyk & Slomski 2016) and involved also MA English philology students of the University of Łódź. In the course of the subsequent semesters, the cooperation has been supervized by Saveena Veeramoothoo of the University of Minnesota and the present author.

There were 10–25 Polish students each semester engaged in the cooperation and a similar number of American students. The Polish students are all native speakers of Polish, of varied background, majoring in English studies (English philology) and at the same time, completing their specialized translation programme. During the current term (winter semester 2019) a group of 8 Polish

Konin MA students, majoring in Foreign Languages in Media & Business, joined the collaborative team.

The Polish students' proficiency in English, evaluated according to the criteria of *The Common European Framework of Reference for Languages*, ranges between B1 and C1 levels, i.e., between so-called independent user's *threshold* or *intermediate* proficiency or *vantage or intermediate* proficiency in English, on the one hand, and *effective operational or advanced* proficiency, on the other. All of the UMN students are native speakers of English and the common majors among them are engineering, business and economics, health and anthropology.

American and Polish students are first paired by the instructors and the Polish students perform two distinct types of task during the first and the second terms. In the first (winter) term the Polish students select their own texts in Polish, typically a press article, involving local culture-specific phenomena or events, and produce an argumentative essay in English on the theme of the article and email them to their US collaborators. In a series of email exchanges aimed at the grammatical and lexical feedback of the English used by the Polish students and the clarification of Polish cultural terms, the Polish students introduce a number of modifications and submit the final version of the essay, forwarding them to their American pair-partners and to their UMN and Polish instructors.

During the second term (summer semester) Polish students perform the same type of task the American students perform in both semesters. For this assignment, peer editing groups collaborate to complete four tasks. First, each participant creates a set of instructions. Once they have a draft of those instructions, the students design and perform a usability test and each Polish and American student forwards the instruction to his/her relevant pair-partner. The partner reads the instruction, proposes revision when needed, and sends the usability comments to the partner. The collaborating students revise their instructions based on feedback from the usability test and send them back to the partner student. The partner students produce objects according to the instruction, document the work and compose a memo that describes how the instructions are rhetorically effective and how they were shaped by one's usability testing. In this memo they also describe the partner pairs' role in creating the instructions and users testing them. The timetable proposed is with firm deadlines. The pairs can draft instructions using Google Docs.

Upon the completion of the task all collaborators are asked to fill in a short post-task survey and write a narrative reflective memo. As the survey involves only ranking answers from predetermined response sets, the data discussed in the present paper are excerpted only from the students' corrective feedback and from the Reflective memos.

To sum up the procedure, the discussed collaborative project engages e-tandem and blended intercultural models (Godwin-Jones 2019: 9), in which speakers of Polish and English are paired to engage in asynchronous collaborative tasks, which also involve some preparation and collaboration between classes and instructors and discussing the experiences both in-class and online.

The aims of the project, in which one party is represented by native speakers of the working language, while the other is represented by non-native speakers are twofold. As other authors engaged in the TAPP project propose (Humbley et. al. 2005; www.NDSU/English/Trans-Atlantic and Pacific Project) "cooperation with EFL students may help instructors to inform native speakers in their classroom about the necessity to adjust writing for the needs of non-native audience." On the other hand, the NNS benefit from the native linguistic and cultural knowledge of the NS, which helps the NNS to improve their working language proficiency.

4. Research methodology

US and PL students' collaboration has taken place for over eight semesters (2015–2020), as specified in more detail in Section 3. above. Each cooperative team exchanged email letters, comments and consecutive versions of the texts circulating between the Polish and US students during all the cooperation stages. All files were forwarded (cc) to both the US and Polish teachers. The students have access to these comments and typically get additional feedback in person from the lecturers either during final meetings or at the consultation periods. The materials produced by all US-Polish partner-pairs throughout each of the semesters have been collected in terms of three categories: (1) email texts, (2) consecutive versions of the essays (2 versions by each pair-partner on average), (3) post-task surveys. 20 samples from each of the collaborative periods were selected (10 from PL and 10 from US) to exemplify claims discussed in the present study in terms frequency counts of relevant discourse strategies as well as types of peer correction and discourse structures.

The research methodology involves also the students' reflections on their collaboration, their surveys and online interaction, which are taken as additional research materials with regard to judgment and argumentation strategies they use in essays and tasks they were performing during the period of collaboration.

5. Corrective feedback

Corrective feedback is typically understood as "a more competent speaker's reaction to learners' ill-formed output" (Panova & Lyster, 2002). The vast literature on foreign language errors assumes two types of error from the point of view of the topic of the present study. The first are overt errors, grammatical syntactic and phraseological – the other – covert ones, referring to inadequate communication and discourse practices (Corder 1971, Brown 2007) in language acquisition processes.

Foreign language acquisition and error correction strategies used in various groups of learners and different contexts have been subject to analyses for years now (e.g., Arabski 1979), stimulating research and hypotheses with regard to different types of learning and acquisition (Schmidt 1990, Ellis 2007, 2009; Rabiej 2015). Online foreign language instruction and learning (e-learning) has also been subject to numerous studies and analyses (e.g., Turula 2018, Krajka 2001). Error correction is an indispensable part and parcel of the acquisition process (Pawlak 2009: 328, 2013), as it makes possible noticing and identification of the questionable forms and negotiation of a more correct outcome, as foregrounded in Long's *Interaction Hypothesis* (1996). Both feedback defined as *corrective recast* (direct corrections and providing correct forms) or *metalinguistic* feedback (applying a more descriptive strategy) (Monteiro 2014) have their advantages and drawbacks, although in the context of the collaborative tasks analysed in the present paper we observe that direct corrections are avoided with regard to the narrative type of corrective comment by both native and non-native students.[1] The situation is different in the case of direct in-text corrections made during the exchange discussed in the present study. Other circumstances relevant for the discussed corrective feedback concern the phenomenon of politeness and politeness strategies. First of all, online interaction is less direct than e.g., face-to-face interaction, especially as the American and Polish students never met before. Thus, it can be assumed that it is primarily politeness considerations that would decide about the use of metalinguistic feedback rather than direct corrective recast in the narrative context. Another reason may be associated with a fairly short corrective experience of either of the two groups of students, i.e., their rather low level of certainty with regard to some types of language inaccuracies. This primarily refers to non-language students of UMN, who are non-language students and the TAPP collaboration

1 See Lewandowska-Tomaszczyk and Slomski (2016) for a more extensive discussion of peer corrective feedback.

was one of the first of their tasks with reference to correcting linguistic inadequacies. In the case of Polish students, all of them did have some teacher training before, which makes the situation more familiar to them. Nevertheless, their position as non-native users of English, as well as clearly lower language competences, particularly when confronted with native speakers, exerts an unfavourable impact on their position in the interaction. In both cases, it is the role of *face work* that is at issue in such contexts.

6. Identity

Linguistic identity is a combination of *language expertise*, *language affiliation*, and *language inheritance*, *a relationship between one's sense of self and a means of communication*, by referring to multiple language practices, in different contexts (Lewandowska-Tomaszczyk 2020). In the context of intercultural cooperation both groups develop what can be dubbed *pluricultural identities* which, similarly to the concept of Block's *plurilinguistic identity* (2007: 27), involves, "socially constructed, self-conscious, ongoing narratives that individuals perform, interpret and project in dress, bodily movements, actions and language," while in the context of online communication, covers in particular better understanding of peers from different cultures. Each of the aspects of culture co-occurs with a number of parameters, such as the social class, generation and gender as well as language and education.

7. Argumentation and face work

One potentially *face threating act* (Goffman 1967) is to present a product of one's own work to the scrutiny of others. A number of communicative strategies that can lower face threat and facilitate upholding one's face, social prestige and personal pride are face-saving politeness strategies that are used in discourse to avoid one's own or the addressee's humiliation or embarrassment, to maintain one's dignity or preserve one's reputation (Brown & Levinson 1987). Direct recast strategy is much more face-threatening than metalinguistic recast from this point of view. Therefore, all argumentative explanations and explications, as well as threat-weakening phraseology are typically used by students in their corrective feedback to mitigate the corrective feedback and make possible to uphold the interactant's (collaborating partner's) face.

From this point of view, it seems of special importance on the part of the native language student to be particularly attentive to their interlocutor's face work.

That such a politeness strategy is effective is confirmed in Polish students' post-task reflections on the collaboration with the American peers:

(1) It was nice to see that a native speaker enjoyed and appreciated my essay. Even though teachers' positive comments always make me feel better about my skills, it was especially great to hear such comments from a native speaker of English.

8. Introducing oneself in TAPP

The asymmetric language competences characterizing native – non-native speaker collaboration are re-enforced by more general cultural-linguistic differences. Although similar to Polish from the point of view of emotion and affect expressivity, American politeness is grounded in a smaller social distance type of context than the Polish one. This is visible both in the strategies employed when introducing oneself as well as, which will be exemplified in the next sections of the present paper, in the higher number of direct, friendly ways the American students employ in their critical comments on the Polish students' writing when juxtaposed to the Polish politeness practices in such cases.

(2) NNS to NS[2]
My name in XX [first name].[3] I am 22 years old. I live in XX. It is a small city located in central Poland. I am a M.A. student in the Department of Translation Studies at the University of Lodz. I am interested in applied linguistics. I love teaching English to young learners. I like listening to music and watching thriller movies.
I am glad to be working with you.
I am sending you my translation. Feel free to correct any mistakes. If you have any questions or comments, please let me know.
Sincerely,
XX

(3) ANSWER to (2) – NS to NNS
Hello XX [first name],
It was incredibly nice getting to know you. I was fascinated to hear how different Poland is from America. I was especially interested in the tradition of smiling because it is so programmed here in America to gently smile to others as you pass by to show neighborliness. It did not even occur to me that my whole life I have been graciously grinning at strangers. A little about me, is my name is Jake J. and I am 18 years old. I live near the Twin Cities (Minneapolis/Saint Paul) of Minnesota. I attend North Dakota State University and would like to major in electrical engineering

2 The abbreviation NNS is used for non-native speakers/students, while NS – for native speakers/students. All students' texts are quoted in the original linguistic form.
3 All personal information in the students' texts is anonymized.

with a minor in computer science. I love Mexican food and my favorite place in the whole is my lake home up north in Minnesota. I do, like you, enjoying listening to music and highly recommend checking out Apple Music! I like to watch most types of movies, but I really like comedies and adventure.

A few of the American students collaborating with the Polish ones are older and more experienced, they are also employed as teaching assistants at their University, like the one in (4) below. This may be one of the reasons why their attitude to a foreign student is particularly warm and full of understanding. The student in (4) is keen to provide her judgment on the cooperation, makes her expectation and arguments clear and well structured (e.g., *In terms of addressing potential barriers, I do expect a small amount whether that is technical, language/communication, and/or differences between countries…*).[4]

(4) NS to NNS
Hi XX,
Thank you for sending your Pre-Learning Report! This is helpful information to know so that I can understand who you are and what your background is. […]
My name is XX and I am 21 years old. *I am a female and my pronouns are she/her/hers.* Before attending the University of Minnesota, I graduated high school in *Chicago is where I am from and grew up in.[…] *I have a variety of work experiences.* […] *I currently work as a Teaching Assistant for an online class, titled XX.*
In terms of addressing potential barriers, I do expect a small amount whether that is technical, language/communication, and/or differences between countries. For instance, I believe that Poland is about 7 hours ahead of the United States. For instance, I am sending this email pretty late at night (around 11:45PM), but you will be receiving it around 6:45am!! *This might be a technical barrier that we will have to keep in mind. In addition, any slang I might use should be kept at a minimum to avoid confusion (barriers in communication). Even differences such as how temperature is measured/recorded between countries could be a small barrier in terms of how we write.* […] I look forward to collaborating with you and creating this international, professional relationship!

9. Error correction comments

Error correction and comments are performed in two ways. They are either discussed in the main body of mutual mail texts in terms of more narrative comments or else they are inserted into the original texts using the 'track changes' function.

4 The argumentative parts are italicized in the examples throughout the whole paper.

9.1. Narrative error correction

There are significant differences in the style of narrative error correction comments between native and non-native language students. The differences refer first of all to the length of the comments, introduction of the arguments and face work.

(5) Examples of NNS to NS corrective feedback
(i)
NS's essay: *The best way to stop college freshman from gaining weight is to try and get them to live a healthy lifestyle.*
NNS's comment: What do you think about a little change into: "The best way to stop college freshmen from gaining weight is to get them to live a healthy lifestyle?"
NS's response: Yes, I agree that "freshmen" works better.
(ii)
NS's essay: *We will be able to prevent college freshmen from not only gaining weight but also stop them from living an unhealthy lifestyle which would prevent them from doing the best work that they could do while they attend college.*
NNS's comment: What would you say about putting it this way: "We will be able to prevent college freshmen not only from gaining weight but also to stop them from living an unhealthy lifestyle, which would prevent them from doing the best work they could do at college?"
NS's response: Yes I agree to this change it make the sentence sound more smooth.
(iii)
NS's essay: *Eating breakfast will make you feel more full throughout the day so you will not have to eat as much at your other meals.*
NNS's comment: What do you think about writing "fuller" instead of "more full"?
NS's response: I'm not sure. I believe "more full" works well but I can also see "fuller" working too.

The NNS make an attempt to employ polite strategies in their error correction feedback (question strategy *What do you think of...?*, using diminutives (*a little change*), which also seems to have an impact on the rather laconic responses of the native language students. However, the latter typically enrich their answers with some argumentation. The US pair partners' corrective feedback is usually longer than that of the Polish students as exemplified in (6)

(6) Examples of NS to NNS corrective feedback
(i)
I loved reading your paper and learned so much. As I mentioned, it was interesting to learn the differences in tradition and culture of our countries. Your paper was very well written and had an ironically relevant topic, which made it easy for me to understand. You had great vocabulary, in fact, there were a few words I had to google because I did not know the meaning of them. *The grammar and punctuation was good, but I added a*

few recommendations that may be helpful for the future. Lastly, the format of the paper was done very well and the transitions were clear.
(ii)
I think that this was a great beginning for you essay! Although after reading through it, I am still not 100 % sure what the assignment was supposed to be on.
(iii)
I was impressed with your ability to know certain phrases such as: every fiber within him. There are times when the writing is a bit choppy and doesn't seem to flow naturally. I found myself having to reread sentences and felt as though you were jumping to different scenes. [...]
Overall I really enjoyed reading this! I think that it was just a little unclear as to what I was reading.

By providing fairly elaborate argumentation (italicized text in the three samples of (6)) and balancing the positive and corrective comments, most often in terms of indirect Speech Acts rather than direct corrections (e.g., *I think that if you add a paragraph in the beginning to describe what your paper is about exactly it should help*), the native speakers' comments and responses seem much better suited to apply to stimulating their US partners for an extra effort and development of the positive attitude to their linguistic competences.

9.2. NS to NNS in-text corrective feedback

The in-text corrective feedback – by both groups – includes more numerous direct recast corrections and fairly limited argumentation as in (7) below, in which out of 7 in-text corrections, 6 are direct recasts, mitigated by the possibility modal *can* (1 is a bare direct recast in the imperative form). The longest correction ("*Sentence establishing credibility...*") provides more elaborate argumentation. Furthermore, it is strongly mitigated by the modal *might* and the minimizing modifier *a little*). This is obviously conditioned by the "track changes" in-text correction function but even in such contexts the native language students maintain the face-saving strategies, using most often the possibility modality of *can* within the direct recast corrections as in (7) below.

(7) In-text corrections NS to NNS

The human migration that occurred a thousand and five hundred years ago had an impact on the shape of the present-day Europe

The consequence of the great human migration that occurred a thousand and five hundred years ago - that is visible today - is the political division of Europe. Amongst scientists there are constant disputes over the matter of how that turbulent period of history looked like within the boundaries of the present territory of Poland.

According to Andrzej Michałowski, PhD, from the Institute of Prehistory (IP), UAM, Poznan, the extraordinary mobility of peoples is rooted in our human nature. "That perseverance regarding travelling, undoubtedly inherited from the first wandering ancestor of ours, that is homo erectus, basically creates the whole human history. Starting from the very moment of forming our species in Africa, circa two hundred thousand years ago, until the contemporary times, as we observe another great exoduses from the early 20th century." - explains the scientist who deals with the Migration Period on a daily basis. This way the sequence of events that was present in Europe from the 4th to 7th century is defined.

Michałowski summarized the topic from the perspective of research excavation in Wielkopolska in an article "After, before, or in between," which was published in a periodical "The Studies on the Early Poland" (Vol. 4), released by the Museum of the Polish State Origins in Gniezno.

Komentarz [MC1]: You can omit the "and" it's not needed in numbers

Komentarz [MC2]: Can change the "a" to "one"

Komentarz [MC3]: You can get rid of this "and" as well for the same reason

Komentarz [MC4]: Can change "that" to "this" as it is your main subject

Komentarz [MC5]: Sentence establishing credibility to the quoted person, adding "explained" to a 5 line quote is pushing the limit a little. You might want to cut out "explains the scientist who" and just refer to them by name again.

Komentarz [MC6]: Change "an" to" the or his/her"

Generally, as seen in the example in (7), the in-text corrections are mostly of direct recast comments (e.g., *Change "an" to "the" or "his/her"*), although short explanatory arguments are frequently also provided.

In the case of out-of-text corrections, of a more descriptive or narrative type, it is the American students that are more attentive to avoid face-threatening acts by providing, often fairly elaborate, argumentation to their (positive and negative) comments. The Polish students are much more direct. Their comments are shorter and frequently devoid of further explanation or arguments, although – noticeably – they also attempt to employ polite correction strategies. In a few cases in which the Polish students try to expand their corrective comments by providing arguments for their corrections (7 cases in the selected samples), they tend to make reference to grammar books and dictionaries (as in (8) *according to the Oxford dictionary*) – in other words they appeal to authority rather than to their own language competences.

(8)

Water is one of human beings' most basic needs. A shortage of water is a problem that shouldn't be taken lightly. Studies that have been conducted in the last 15 years show that drought conditions in the Red River Valley would lead to a major water deficit. Citizens of the Valley need a plan in place for the worst case scenario. The most logical and feasible solution is to bring water from the Missouri River to the area.

The problem the Red River Valley (and most of North Dakota) faces is an over dependence on surface water as its only sustainable source. The population of the Red River Valley is steadily growing along with its economy which puts further strain on the Red River and its tributaries as a source of water. If a drought were to occur, hundreds of thousands of people

Komentarz [Rec1]: I would say "necessities". I think water is not a need, it is necessary to satisfy our different needs, it is necessary for us to live

Komentarz [Rec2]: I guess you shouldn't use contracted forms in an essay (excluding citations)– but I don't know what are the requirements

Komentarz [Rec3]: "Overdependence" – according to the Oxford dictionary is written together

Another observation refers to lack of Polish students' competences to nuance their linguistic behaviour in the case of eliminating or weakening face threat to the interactant, although some attempts are observed in terms of addressing the partner with an introductory mitigating phrase (e.g., *What would you say about putting it this way…*) and the application of what corresponds to Polish diminutive forms (e.g., *What do you think about <u>a little change</u> into …*). What seems also worth noting is the fact that American students provide their comments in the form of longer descriptive or narrative texts, while the Polish students' preference is to focus on a larger number of smaller grammatical and stylistic matters.

10. Arguments in reflective memos

Other materials to analyse judgment and argumentation structures as applied by the collaborating students are narrative-style reflective memos the students are asked to write upon completion of all the tasks. In the present section an analysis of argument structure in selected memos of American (NS) and Polish (NNS) students is presented.

(9) *Reflective memos* [excerpted fragments]

Reflective memo NNS 1

I decided to prepare a recipe: how to make pizza at home. […] *I created these documents in the style of handouts because this form is easy to be followed and it is most popular for recipes. First, I wrote short introduction and caution because these instructions are created for adults and some steps may be dangerous for young children; due to the fact that warm water is used and there is a necessity to heat the oven, which may be unsafe for children.*

Reflective memo 2 NNS

Since handout is the most frequently met form for recipes, constructing mine in such a structure seemed to be the most understandable option. A […] *I chose specifically those images as I believed their adding can compensate what the verbal instructions did not express.*

Reflective memo NS 3

The airplane that I chose is called "Origami plane" and it is a fast flying one. [...] Since the folding requires a lot of precision and use of scissors I think that the person who is going to prepare the plane should be at least 12 years old. Second, I thought that the written description of particular steps would not be enough. That is why I decided to fold the plane one more time and take photos of every single step.

Reflective memo 4 NS

My topic was making my favorite type of muffins, and I was able to dissect my topic into steps, since that's how food is made. [...] I think these muffins were able to be replicated very easy because I broke down the steps to one action per step.

Reflective memo 6 NS

I decided on the process of making an envelope out of common household materials. [...] After choosing the topic of how to make an envelope, I asked myself many questions: 1. Who would use these instructions? 2. Why is this important? 3. What should be included in the instructions? 4. Where and when will these instructions be used? I considered these questions when explaining each step of the process and while writing a short introduction paragraph to hook the readers.

The reflective memos present considerably less variance in the judgment argument structure between native – non-native styles than the introductory parts and error correction tasks. Both native and non-native students logically order all relevant steps in their tasks to expose reasons for a particular sequence of the required stages. It seems that both the fact that the memos follow the tasks personally performed by each of the students, that each of the students prepares a usability report, documents the work and collaborates with their UMN partner throughout the whole task, contributed to the quality of both the final writing assignment and – what seems to be of particular importance – to the high quality of the product made according to the instructions.

11. Conclusions: Cultural markers in judgment expression and argumentation

Cross-cultural and individual differences in judgment and argument expression in the period of collaborative tasks between Polish and American students are – to a large extent – a consequence of the difference between the respective student experiences, their cultural and linguistic identities.

The properties of the two cultures the students are exposed to contribute to the development of their pluricultural and plurilinguistic identities. All of them create a unique cluster of properties constituting one *Gestalt* of a particular individual identity. Under the influence of the student's contact with a foreign language and culture, his/her reactions, behaviour and judgments are likely to develop to accommodate the new values and judgments. This exercise also helps native language students to understand better the task they were working on themselves:

> ...even though we are different and in different parts of the world, there are things that are similar between us [...] I feel like the point of this project was to work on creating a document with clarity and allowing the reader to understand something that could be a completely foreign concept to them. I feel like through taking into consideration that me and my partner come from different cultures it helped me take a more in depth look into the document I was creating (from a reflective memo by an American student).

While the American students typically use friendly comments for corrections, the Polish students' remarks convey suggestions by reference to authority (dictionaries/grammar books) rather than to their addressees' native language and their own acquired competences. In the present study it is exposure and reference to grammar books and dictionaries, academic writing and texts visible in the Polish group in the contacts with the American students; which makes the Polish students shape part of their own writing identity (see also Lehman 2018).

The differences in the narrative error correction comments between native and non-native language students are particularly demonstrated in the US students' more varied style of introducing themselves to their Polish pair partners, longer comments, more individualized types of error correction arguments and more salient markers of respecting their partners' face (a higher number of mitigating moves).

Notwithstanding the fact that resort to authority, dictionaries or grammar books in this case, may involve diverse causes and background, it can be considered an outcome of some kind of interactional asymmetry, conditioned either by different cultural models or by unequal discourse power distribution in the communicative context. On the one hand, the American students have native experience with English, which makes them a dominant party in the interaction. On the other hand, it is the Polish students, studying for their MA in translation and in media and business communication, that are more experienced in metalinguistic reflection and error correction.

Other aspects that cannot be left out unappreciated is the positive function of the collaborative experience, particularly demonstrated in the reflective memos, rooted in the fact that the students' assignment was fully practical task oriented. What also needs to be mentioned is the position and function of the lecturer in such contexts. The role of "guided reflection" in virtual collaboration is particularly important for developing appreciation of solid argument-based peer error correction. Telecollaboration plays a significant role and creates opportunities for exposure to different strategies of mutual face work and respect with regard to peers of different cultural backgrounds. And yet, as discussed in Turula and Reith (2015), or Lewandowska-Tomaszczyk (2019), intercultural telecollaborative student contacts must be set up with care for various reasons, among others, to avoid strengthening negative cultural stereotypes in the collaborating teams, and, furthermore, as quoted after Godwin-Jones (2019:8), because "linguistic and intercultural gains are by no means automatic."

References

Arabski, J. (1979). *Errors as Indications of the Development of Interlanguage.* Katowice: Wydawnictwo Uniwersytetu Śląskiego.

Block, D. (2007). *Second Language Identities.* London: Continuum.

Brown, H.D. (2007). *Principles of Language Learning and Teaching.* White Plains, NY: Pearson Education.

Brown, P. & Levinson, S.C. (1987). *Politeness: Some Universals in Language Usage.* Cambridge: Cambridge University Press.

Corder, S. (1971). Idiosyncratic dialects and error analysis. *International Review of Applied Linguistics.* 5: 147–159.

Ellis, R. (2009). Corrective feedback and teacher development. *L2 Journal, 1*, 3–18.

Ellis, R. (2007). The differential effect of corrective feedback on two grammatical structures. In A. Mackey (Ed.), *Conversational Interaction in Second Language Acquisition* (pp. 339–360). Oxford: Oxford University Press.

Gilbert, M. (2004). Emotion, Argumentation and Informal Logic. *Informal Logic, 24* (3), 245–264.

Godwin-Jones, R. (2019). Telecollaboration as an approach to developing intercultural communication competence. *Language Learning & Technology, 23*(3), 8–28.

Goffman, E. (1967). *Interaction Ritual: Essays in Face to Face Behavior.* New York: Doubleday.

Hinton, M. (2019). Language and argument: a review of the field. *Research in Language, 17*(1), 93–103.

Hofstede, G. (2001). *Consequences: Comparing Values, Behaviors, Institutions, and Organizations Across Nations.* Thousand Oaks, CA: Sage Publications.

Humbley, J., Maylath, B., Mousten, B., Vandepitte, S. & L. Veisblat (2005). Learning localization through Trans-Atlantic collaboration. In G. F. Hayhoe (Ed.), *Proceedings of the IEEE International Professional Communication Conference*, (pp. 578–595). New York: IEEE.

Krajka, J. (2001). Online lessons – Using the Internet to help the coursebook. In K. Cameron (Ed.), *CALL – the Challenge of Change* (pp. 151–159). Exeter: Elm Bank Publications.

Lehman, I. M. (2018). *Authorial Presence in English Academic Texts: A Comparative Study of Student Writing Across Cultures and Disciplines.* Bern: Peter Lang Verlag.

Lewandowska-Tomaszczyk, B. (2020). Spaces of meanings and translators' identities. https://journals.umcs.pl/lsmll/issue/archive *Lublin Studies in Modern Languages and Literature* (online edition).

Lewandowska-Tomaszczyk, B. (2019). Identity dynamics in student contacts with foreign languages and cultures." In E. W. Popova (Ed.), *Society and Laguages in the Third Millenium – Communication, Education, Translation* (pp. 153–177). Moscow: RUDN.

Lewandowska-Tomaszczyk, B. & Slomski, H. (2016). Collaboration in language development between American and Polish university students. *Konin Language Studies*, *4/3*, 305–330.

Long, M. H. (1996). The role of the linguistic environment in second language acquisition. In W. Ritchie & T. Bhatia (Eds.), *Handbook of Second Language Acquisition* (pp. 413–468). San Diego: Academic Press Inc.

Maylath, B., Vandepitte, S., Minacori, P., Isohella, S., Mousten, B. & J. Humbley (2013). Managing complexity: A technical communication translation case study in multilateral international collaboration. *Technical Communication Quarterly*, *22*, 67–84.

Monteiro, K. (2014). Corrective feedback during video-conferencing. *Language Learning and Technology*, *18* (3), 56–79.

Panova, I. & Lyster, R. (2002). Patterns of Corrective Feedback and Uptake in an Adult ESL Classroom. *TESOL Quarterly*, *36/4*, 573–595.

Pawlak, M. (2013). Czynniki warunkujące występowanie i skuteczność korekty błędów językowych podczas mówienia. In M. Pawlak (Ed.), *Mówienie w języku obcym: skuteczne uczenie się, nauczanie i ocenianie* (pp. 305–326). Poznań–Kalisz–Konin: Wydział Pedagogiczno-Artystyczny UAM w Poznaniu.

Pawlak, M. (2009). Rola nauczyciela w kształtowaniu procesów interakcyjnych w klasie językowej. In M. Pawlak, A. Mystkowska-Wiertelak & A. Pietrzykowska (Eds.), *Nauczyciel języków obcych dziś i jutro* (pp. 311–337). Poznań–Kalisz: Wydział Pedagogiczno-Artystyczny UAM w Poznaniu.

Rabiej, A. (2015). Podejścia do błędów i ich poprawy we współczesnej glottodydaktyce. *Acta Universitatis Lodziensis. Kształcenie polonistyczne cudzoziemców, 22*, 61–73.

Schmidt R. (1990). The role of consciousness in second language learning. *Applied Linguistics, 11*, 17–46.

TAPP PROJECT, North Dakota State University - Paris Diderot University procedure https://www.ndsu.edu/english/transatlantic_and_pacific_translations/www.NDSU/English/Trans-Atlantic and Pacific Project

Turula, A. (2018). *E-learning akademicki. Perspektywa humanistyczna*. Kraków: Wydawnictwo Naukowe Uniwersytetu Pedagogicznego.

Turula, A. & Raith, Th. (2015). Telecollaboration insights: learning from exchanges that fail. *The EuroCALL Review* 23:2. 19–37. https://polipapers.upv.es/index.php/eurocall/article/view/4666/4793

Anita Buczek-Zawiła

Pedagogical University, Kraków, Poland

Supporting instruction in English pronunciation with CALL: a blended-learning component in English Phonetics course at undergraduate level

Abstract: The curriculum for undergraduate English studies in Poland includes courses in English phonetics and pronunciation, the primary objective of which is to train students to achieve a high level of pronunciation competence in English. Students are also instructed in the mechanisms of speech production, classification of speech sounds and principles of IPA transcription, with the belief that familiarity with these elements will result in more conscious sound perception, discrimination and production. Today these skills can be taught with the use of digital tools. By choosing to follow a blended-learning course format the teacher incorporates the elements of CALL/CAPT into the teaching in a more structured manner. This creates the opportunities to provide a more varied, multisensory and multi-channelled and easily available training. Such organization will be supplementary to but correlated with what happens in face-to-face class instruction. An example of such a hybrid course, running for several years in the English Studies Department at the Pedagogical University of Kraków for Year 1 students, is presented in the chapter. It involves a number of diverse activities, strengthening the students' competence in sound perception and production, at the same time gradually accustoming them to elements of ICT to appear more prominently as their degree progresses.

Keywords: pronunciation, metacompetence, CALL, CAPT, blended-learning

1. Introduction

The English Studies in Poland characteristically place high importance on developing the students' language skills in addition to promoting academic excellence in other philological subjects. The curricula, therefore, obligatorily include courses in English phonetics and pronunciation, with various numbers of hours allocated at different semesters. The objective of these courses is to train students to achieve a high, near native-like level of pronunciation in English. In addition, students are instructed in the principles of IPA phonetic transcription, basic speech production mechanisms, and classification of speech sounds, with the belief that familiarity with these background elements will result in more conscious sound perception, discrimination, and production.

However, the primary objective of these courses remains to improve the students' actual pronunciation of English and thus reducing L1– accentedness. Explicit lessons in L2 phonetics have been shown to corroborate the development of better sound discrimination and production abilities. The effect of face-to-face phonetics instruction is believed to be directly enhanced by other pedagogical alternatives, CALL-related ones among them. An amalgam of mutually-complementary teaching measures appears to work best towards achieving the desirable competence and micro-skill level, including a substantial component of metacompetence-oriented instruction to promote L2 (here: English) phonological acquisition (Wrembel 2005).

The chapter begins by presenting a state-of-the art review of subject literature, pertaining to techniques and measures currently employed in regular university phonetics courses, discussing possible extra components incorporated via hybrid course organization. It later presents a project of one such course, variously called (Practical) (English) Phonetics, developed and run successfully in the English Studies department at the Pedagogical University of Kraków. In conclusion, the paper provides arguments to support the proposed course organization.

2. Review of literature

2.1. CALL and pronunciation training

Computer Assisted Language Learning (CALL) has raised substantial hopes among educators as to the assistance it can offer in the area of both effective and attractive foreign language instruction. These hopes have been particularly high when pronunciation training is taken into consideration – Computer Assisted Pronunciation Training (CAPT) appeared to be potentially the most fruitful area of new technologies application (Levis 2007). It is believed that computer- and web-based applications and programs are particularly suited here as they provide accessible, individualized instruction. This is achieved also through auditory discrimination and repetition tasks, automatic visual support which demonstrates to learners how closely they approximated the set standard[1] (Lewis 2007). While CAPT undoubtedly exhibits flexibility and involves

1 Even though they seem to fail to give students adequate, accurate and meaningful feedback.

valuable varied instructional modes, it is also true that is comprises of certain more or less evident difficulties in terms of pedagogical measures, technological limitations, and teacher-preparedness. In regular courses that specifically target foreign language pronunciation taking a number of pedagogically-sound measures to enrich and enhance instruction appears a viable pre-requisite. These measures at all levels, including academia, may – and perhaps ought to – involve ICT and generally conceived of digital literacies.

The literacies can be developed and practiced via a number of in-classroom and out-of-classroom techniques. Web-based pronunciation practice has been growing in popularity over the years, with a variety of applications and websites developed commercially or as open resources. These are used to work on discriminating, practicing and producing target language sounds, implemented both as in-class and for self-study (Krajka 2006). Additional benefits of incorporating elements of CALL/CAPT have been pointed out in Harper (2004); among them the observation that CALL can reduce stress and anxiety often associated with learning and producing more accurate pronunciation, it allows students in larger classes to receive important individual feedback immediately. Because it is normally interactive, it thereby makes the learning experience more enjoyable for both the instructor and the student.

Although the popular opinion is that technology is there to stay when it comes to pronunciation teaching, some teachers (and researchers) express discomfort with such innovations, pointing to difficulties with their implementation and use, and voicing some fears as to the possibility of the instructor being replaced by technology. The CAPT appliances are not to be understood only as employing computers, no matter how useful and facilitative they are (Gilakjani 2016; Gilakjani & Sabouri 2017). Current implementations of technology (broadly conceived of) in pronunciation training, as well as an overview of specially-designed technological elements to be used and possibilities created by those, are discussed in Sobkowiak (2005), Eskenazi (2009), and much updated in O'Brien et al. (2018). To mention one important aspect, they can offer High Variability Phonetic Training (Barriuso and Hayes-Harb 2018) on a regular basis.

However, it has been emphasized on numerous occasions (Levis 2007; Nozawa 2011; Yoshida 2018) that the tool must first of all be appropriate to the assumed learner and teacher objectives, and that it can be used effectively only to the extent the instructor utilizes its many possibilities and implements them successfully (Nozawa 2011). In other words, there needs to be skilful learner-task-tool affordancing. This requires some pedagogical expertise since sometimes the sheer number and variety of available resources may seem overwhelming to the teachers and they need guidance in selecting those that they can use effectively (Yoshida 2018).

2.2. Metacompetence-oriented model of phonological acquisition

The job that is targeted in the project described in later sections of this chapter is to train students of English Studies to develop a near-native like pronunciation of English they need as future professionals (teachers, interpreters, etc.) in a manner that is explanatory enough and thus conducive to learning at the same time. For several years now, researchers have been trying to feed declarative knowledge into building phonetic proficiency (Sobkowiak 2005). That stems from the conviction that "in order to do anything one must have – in varying proportions depending on the actual activity – both the "theoretical" and "practical" competence" (Sobkowiak (2005: 3), which brings about teaching the declarative, explicit "know-that" pertaining to the phonetic/phonological component of the target language. This, in turn, is claimed to corroborate developing the practical competence.

Wrembel (2005) developed an approach she calls metacompence-oriented model of phonological acquisition, which may be the answer to the abovementioned course demands. The model, admittedly geared towards adult learners, proposes to incorporate the knowledge about the sound system of a given language into phonetic classes with the view of enhancing the students' general understanding of how the sound component works. This, in turn, is believed to facilitate discrimination, perception, and ultimately production of target language sounds.

> The metacompetence-oriented model advocates the reliance on the cognitive, and not only motor, aspect of pronunciation training. […] [It] posits that conscious knowledge of phonetics and phonology and developed metalinguistic awareness are related to second language pronunciation achievements. (Wrembel 2005: 1)

The first stage of phonological acquisition involves guided ear-training and consciousness-raising to train the adequate perception of the segmental (and to some extent suprasegmental) contrasts. Effective perception feeds into production, where conscious knowledge of articulation mechanisms is assumed to assist learners' phonetic performance, acting as self-monitoring and feedback-giving device. Consequently, phonological metacompetence is postulated as a major facilitative component enhancing the process of acquisition and ultimately actual sound realizations. Through the combination of multifarious techniques and strategies relating to the cognitive, affective and psycho-motor aspects of pronunciation training, the model tries to take into account also a number of socio- and psycholinguistic conditions, all in addition to oral and auditory capacities.

For any such training to be successful, it must be holistic. In other words, it must be student-centred and concern every student at every level, catering to the needs and abilities of different individuals. The holistic approach encourages students to be critical, confident, and independent. Here, learning is a process of self-improvement that explicitly recognizes the self and the social context of learning and teaching, and it recognizes the needs of the individual learner in the interaction (Argyros 2012). Holistic learning must by nature be polysensory. In phonetics it involves not only imitating the given input as faithfully as one can but also experiencing it through sight, touch, emotions and cognitive processing. That means that good pronunciation comes from practice in articulation, on the one hand, and in auditory perception and cognitive training, on the other.

2.3. The blended learning design

There is a widespread belief that CALL supports both types of knowledge – the declarative and the procedural. Therefore it is seen as a welcome addition to regular face-to-face classroom training. The character of certain courses, particularly those at academia, places huge demands in terms of good procedural performance and therefore treats the inclusion of the technological component as an instance of good pedagogical practices. The technological element that is generally encouraged to be used at tertiary education is an institution-selected Learning Management System (e.g. Moodle) and the formula is that of *blended learning*. A simple definition of this hybrid model is presented below:

> The teaching formula referred to as *blended learning* combines traditional face-to-face classroom interaction with computer-mediated activities and belongs to the most frequently employed options in the process of foreign language teaching. As opposed to pure *e-learning*, it is an outcome of mixing two different learning environments with the view to optimizing the conditions for learning and making it more efficient. (Lesiak-Bielawska 2012: 48)

It is thus clear that in such hybrid courses promote the coexistence of conventional, teacher-supervized instruction with newer, electronic in character, formats and activities (Mokwa-Tarnowska 2015). This has an added asset on drawing off young people tech-comfyness.

Garrison (2011: 113), again, emphasizes that the greatest incursion of e-learning into tertiary education is through the blended learning designs, with its full integration of face-to-face and online activities. It cannot be viewed simply as adding optional or supplementary materials and tasks to what is fundamentally a regular classroom-based learning experience. At the core of the formula is the intent to rethink and perhaps redesign how the course can be best delivered to meet the academic goals. The proportion of non-online and online components and activities must be appropriate to the assumed educational purpose at hand, with the exact percentages being irrelevant. The major advantages of b-learning courses relate to the following (Plebańska & Kula 2011: 19 ff):

- mixed forms of interaction and, as a result, the possibilities of motivating students, directly (in contact) and indirectly (via computer-mediated communication),
- supporting students' individual learning pace and paths,
- more flexibility in terms of didactic content[2] focusing on the new and challenging,
- working at a convenient time and place (student decision) – the *anywhere-anytime* principle,
- dynamic material presentation (multimedia, e-lessons, tests, control questions, etc.),
- working with text, image and sound – which by fulfilling the postulate of polysensory teaching caters to the needs of different types of students' learning styles.

The list presented above underlines the elements that significantly raise the chances of effective training. Needless to say, such course design requires new competences from the tutors, the primary ones among them involve having the skills necessary in order to effectively adapt the conventional teaching methodology to distance learning conditions, to harmonically combine the classroom and the online materials and tasks, as well as being aware of the conditions that determine students' online activity and of the rules governing the individual student work organizations in virtual environment (Smyrnova-Trybulska 2018).[3]

It needs to be emphasized that the LMS of Moodle and the associated blended-learning design can and has successfully been implemented in teaching other

---

2 For instance, by omitting the content or subject matter a student is well versed in, and thus avoiding the potential boredom factor.

3 A full list of teacher competences and micro-skills is available in Smyrnowa-Trybulska (2018: 294 ff).

language skills and subsystems, not only pronunciation, which is the chapter focus. Moodle-based instruction can assist language instruction in general. Sun (2014) presents a case for college-level general English course organized according to the blended-learning formula. His results reveal that the Moodle-based blended learning can greatly improve the language learners' enthusiasm and initiative, effectively enhance the learners' English comprehensive competence and develop their cooperative learning and team spirit. Tsai and Talley (2014) report on the enhancement of (EFL reading) strategy use after running Moodle-supported strategy instruction on both reading comprehension and strategy use among EFL students. Hsieh and Ji (2013), for instance, discuss the advantage of implementing synchronous and asynchronous communications via the CMS of Moodle when training reading comprehension, with learners outperforming others who did not have the benefit of the online component. Bataineh and Mayyas (2017) report similar results for tertiary education level instruction in EFL grammar and reading with the use of hybrid course design, while Wu (2008) recommends working with Moodle when teaching English writing classes at university level, claiming it constitutes the desirable environment for group interaction and pedagogical intervention. Studies like these (and many more) clearly demonstrate the positive effects of running Moodle-based language learning instruction, especially at college level.

The next part of chapter ventures to present a course that observes the above-mentioned qualifications and objectives, and has been successfully running for several years at one of the academic institutions.

3. The project: origin, presentation and discussion

The following section presents an instance of one specific project of a course designed to train students in their English pronunciation skills, at the same time developing their metalinguistic knowledge pertaining to the sound structure of English, and then building on it. The standard teaching of these matters is here expanded with the use of online component, following the blended-learning model of instruction, with the idea of facilitating learning with multichannelled, multisensory instructional techniques.

3.1. The course

At academia, in language studies departments practical pronunciation training is the order of the day. Unsurprisingly, the B.A. degree programme for English Studies at the Pedagogical University of Kraków (henceforth PUK for convenience) contains a two-semester course, in subsequent curriculum modifications variously called (Practical) (English) Phonetics. The course comprises a total of 90 hours of teaching, in the face-to-face mode. Sobkowiak (2005: 3) observes that "the classic core of pronunciation training in the traditional syllabus includes segments, suprasegmentals, fast speech phenomena, graphophonemics, accentual variation." Thus, here too the content relates primarily to segmental and suprasegmental elements of English phonetics, in the articulatory sphere, so that a desirable, (nearly) accent-free pronunciation can be developed. However, in line with the belief explicitly expressed in Wrembel (2005), classificatory and descriptive concepts, supplemented with the basic understanding of English sound structure, are introduced too. All of that is believed to result in students' phonological metacompetence, which, in turn, informs their auditory, discriminatory and finally articulatory efforts. This is seen as a feeding-breeding relationship. Among the themes students are to master are the basic mechanisms of speech production, description and classification of speech sounds, distinctions between the sound segments of English and their positional variants, voicing contrasts and context-driven sound assimilations.[4]

The typical classroom procedure will integrate the above concepts into regular pronunciation instruction. That involves choral, pair and individual practice under the supervision of a subject tutor, based on a model provided by the recorded material[5] as well as the teacher. Students are thus offered an opportunity to focus on the spoken word, good acoustics, privacy (to the extent it is possible) and attention focus.

The actual thematic content of the course is shown in Table 1.

4 Compare the course content as specified in Karta Kursu (the course syllabus), available at https://anglistyka.up.krakow.pl/karty-kursow/

5 The recorded material comprises selected sections/units of two major handbooks: *How Much Wood Would a Woodchuck Chuck. Podręcznik do nauki wymowy języka angielskiego* + CD (Mańkowska et al. 2017) and *How now, brown cow? A Course in the Pronunciation of English* (Ponsonby 1988).

Table 1. Course content (non-chronological).

SEGMENTAL	SOUNDS IN CONTEXT	BACKGROUND
Vowel [e]	English vowels: the length of the vowel vs. the final consonant	Introductory issues: sound and letter, consonant and vowel; language and dialect, standard, online tools; ICT sources
Vowel [æ]; comparison with the vowel [e]	Strong and weak forms of articles and prepositions	Phonemic transcription: pronunciation and spelling, spelling and transcription
Vowel [ɪ]; comparison with the Polish vowel; spelling and pronunciation	Stressed and unstressed syllables	Symbols of the International Phonetic Alphabet (IPA) – vowels, diphthongs and consonants
Vowel [i:]; comparison between [i:] and [ɪ]	Strong and weak forms of auxiliary verbs	Voicing of consonants in English and Polish language
Alveolar stops [t, d]	Pronunciation of the ending "- (e) s"	Phonological opposition, minimal pairs, homophony, homography, homonymy
The palato-alveolars [ʃ, ʒ, ʧ, ʤ]	Word linking (plain, glides, r-liason)	Speech organs: air current: source and direction; larynx: voicing/ voicelessness, glottal closure
Vowels [ʌ] and [ɒ]	Pronunciation of the ending "-ed"	Speech organs: oral, nasal and nasalized sounds; the oral cavity articulation
Vowel [ɑ:]; comparison of vowels [ʌ] and [ɑ:]	[r] in sandhi (linking vs. intrusive "r")	Places and manners of articulation; the vowel type
Vowel [ɔ:]; comparison of vowels [ɒ] and [ɔ:]	Word stress and rhythm	Classifying vowels – vowel diagram, quality, quantity, lip-rounding
Vowels [u:] and [ʊ]	Sentence accent – contribution to structure and meaning	Consonants – general characteristics: classification of consonants; degree/types of organ approximation;
Vowel [ə]	Schwa as target of reduction	Phonemes and allophones
Vowel [ɜ:]; comparison of [ɜ:] and [ə]		
The interdentals [θ, ð]		
English plosive consonants	Types of stop release: no audible, glottal stop, nasal, lateral; stops in clusters	

The articulatory side is taken care of primarily in class, where students cooperate in pairs following teacher's instructions and under close teacher supervision, with immediate feedback.

A standard message students receive in practical pronunciation classes in language studies departments is that what happens in the class itself is only a small part of the amount of practice needed to develop good pronunciation habits, so that actually a lot of additional, out-of-class effort is required. The authors[6] of the course believe strongly that such out-of-class training needs to be structured and guided to achieve its goals of broadening students competencies.

The solution was sought among the distance-learning possibilities made available via the university e-learning platform, namely via Moodle. As an instance of a virtual learning environment (VLE) Moodle functions primarily as course-managing tool (LMS – Learning Management System). It is seen by instructors as useful, since it allows the teacher to monitor each student's online activity, to communicate with them, to deliver the content via an array of multifarious techniques and activities, and to mark their contributions (Mokwa-Tarnowska 2015). The resources uploaded by the teacher as well as activities designed as part of the course provide the means to run the training effectively and efficiently (Plebańska & Kula 2011). The tasks students do in class and those assigned for self-study may and frequently do involve applying the technological innovations: multimedia, websites, distance learning and the like.

Integrating an online component with traditional classroom has the potential to produce positive results. The effectiveness and the results of such combination are dependent not only on the attractiveness of the online materials but on successful communicating why these activities are there in the first place and why the new technologies are used, and what is their added value (Mokwa-Tarnowska 2015). That demands proper restructuring of the whole course design.

3.2. The *blended learning* design

Starting from the academic year 2014/15 the original course in pronunciation of English at PUK has been undergoing constant modifications to bring about the attractive, student-centred, well-integrated online component.[7] It was

6 Apart from the author of the present chapter, the English Phonetics course was co-designed by Piotr Okas, with subsequent contributions of Alicja Witalisz and Agnieszka Piasecka, all from the English Department at Pedagogical University of Kraków.

7 This was only possible thanks to a series of training sessions on the use of Moodle as a VLE and LMS, conducted for English Department Staff Members by Anna Turula at PUK in the academic year 2013/14.

decided at the start that going completely online and distance in a fundamentally practical course like this one is both unnecessary and undesirable, if not downright detrimental to students. At the same time, the philosophy shared by the authors was that the course was to focus on developing oral skills both in terms of authentic fluency and sound accuracy.

In its present shape the course follows the topic-based rather than weekly-grouped organization. The modular structure follows the two semester content specification. The exact order of subjects as well as the tasks and activities associated are every time decided on by the instructor. Such course organization is reflected in the actual make-up of the online component (Fig. 1), available to students at https://moodle1.up.krakow.pl/course/view.php?id=191.[8]

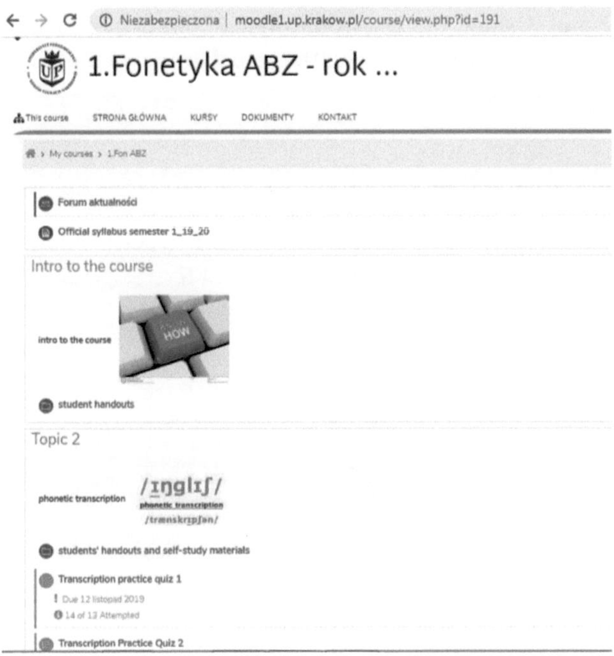

Figure 1. The interface of phonetics course fragment.

8 This is the site where the course resides now. In previous years it was run on the Institute of Modern Languages platform (nf2.up.krakow.pl), but has since been moved according to PUK policies. Some of the illustrations come from this previous site, hence the different layout.

The design incorporates two basic integration patterns (Mokwa-Tarnowska 2015). The first one consists in new content first introduced in class, and subsequently followed/supplemented by tasks basing on it (mostly quizzes). The other model uses the online resources and activities (e.g. the Moodle lesson format) to familiarize the students with new content, to be followed by in-class specific activities that build on this material and frequently expand it. It is the second pattern that implicitly follows the practice of flipped classroom (Turula 2018), where the actual lecture takes the form of an online e-lesson, and the intellectual work stemming from it is transferred into the classroom. The technique allows the student to do the learning at their chosen time and location, and however many times they deem it necessary, with materials being available 24/7. Such individualized practice develops learner autonomy in conditions of maximum personal and psychological security and is conducive to academic development.

Figures 2 and 3 show the classroom-first & online-next pattern, and the flipped classroom design respectively. The actual format of the component tasks is to be discussed presently.

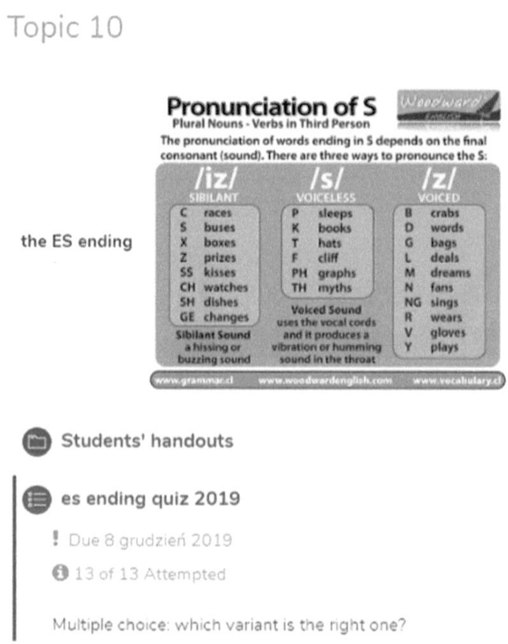

Figure 2. Classroom-first – Moodle-next activity: the ES ending.

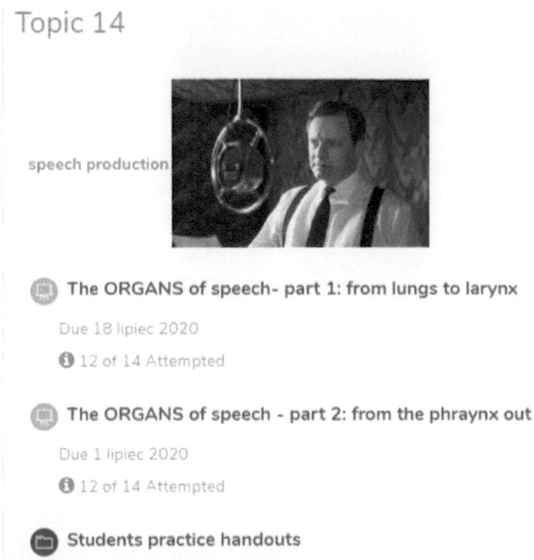

Figure 3. Flipped learning: two online lessons followed by classroom practice: the mechanisms of speech production.

Figure 4 illustrates the case when online e-lecture (the lesson activity) is followed by online activity and only then the work resumes in the conventional classroom based on materials that the tutor made available on Moodle.

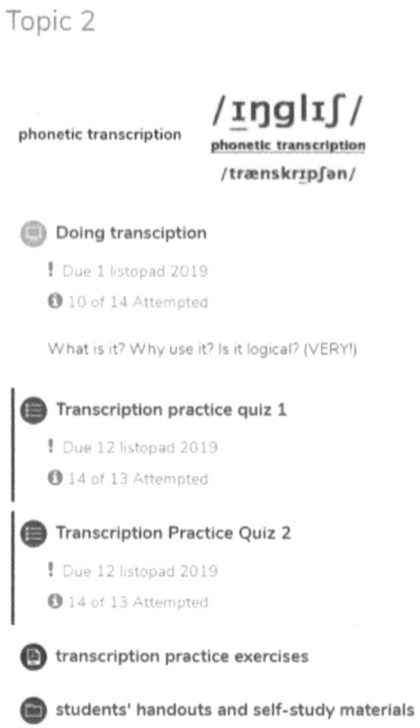

Figure 4. Combined pattern: lesson + online quizzes + classroom practice.

Needless to say, the online platform functions also as a repository of class handouts and practice materials prepared by tutors, or, at a minimum, directing students to relevant portions of the current handbook(s) used. Additionally, the labels featuring in every topic serve a double function: first they act as a visual reminder of what a given topic deals with, and second they are often clickable, directing students to other interesting and valuable web resources they can make use of. This can be a webpage devoted to a given topic and very relevant to what the problem entails, or a video tutorial available elsewhere, as an open resource, provided the material has been previously positively evaluated by the teacher. That ensures that students receive good quality input (examples below). More so, they can experience a variety of presentation modes and pronunciation models. The resources can refer to connected speech practice (Fig. 5), metalinguistic portion of the course (Fig. 6) or to actual peculiarities of English Pronunciation (Fig. 7).

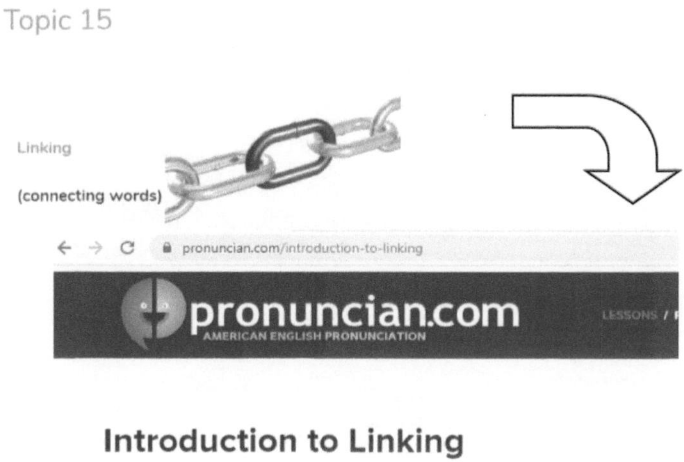

Figure 5. Clickable label: online resource – webpage.

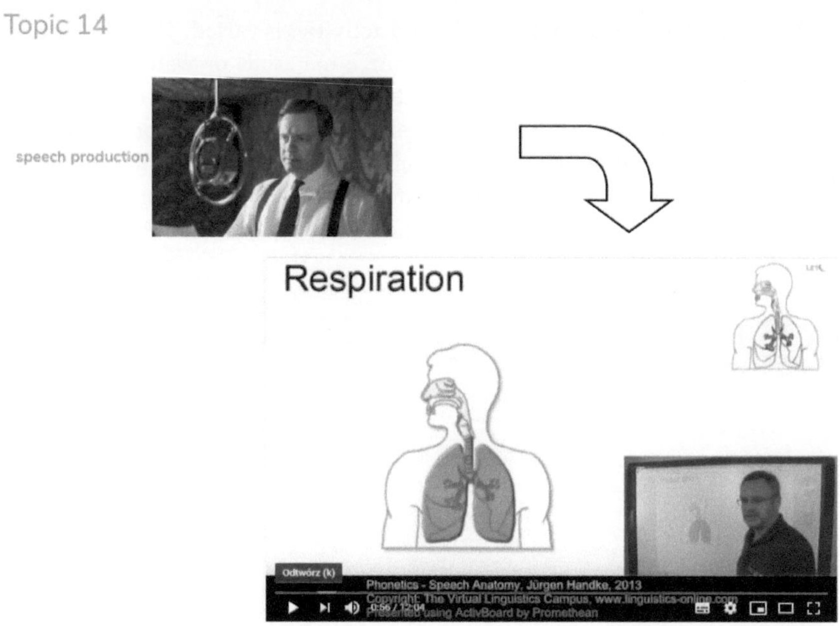

Figure 6. Clickable label: video tutorial.

Listen and practice the names of British cities

- Names of some British cities
- Angliphenia - British city names often mispronounced
- Some differences between British and American words
- Some new English words
- How to pronounce -ed endings

Figure 7. Extra practice in tricky aspects of English pronunciation – web-based practice resources.

The actual structure of online tasks and activities is varied. The tasks involve mostly reading supplementary open resource materials or watching tutorials (Figures 5, 6 and 7). Sometimes short videos, apparently unrelated to the content matter, that is illustrating anatomical rather than articulatory details, are hyperlinked. These are to raise the awareness of students as to the functioning of, for example, the vocal tract or illustrate otherwise abstract concepts such as "vowel space" or "nasal articulation." Figure 8 shows some examples.

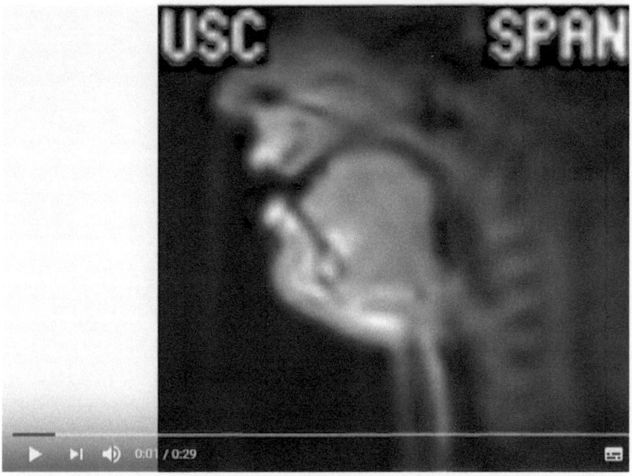

The Flexible Tongue

Figure 8. Non-phonetic awareness-raising videos.

The two activities used primarily as structured online tasks are quizzes and lessons. Let us begin with the first of those. Those used in the course follow varied test formats: multiple-choice, true-false, cloze, drag-and-drop onto text or drag-and-drop onto picture. That way students test-taking skills are activated as well, since the formats keep changing. They are generally based on a text and/or image displayed on the screen. Illustration is provided in Figure 9.

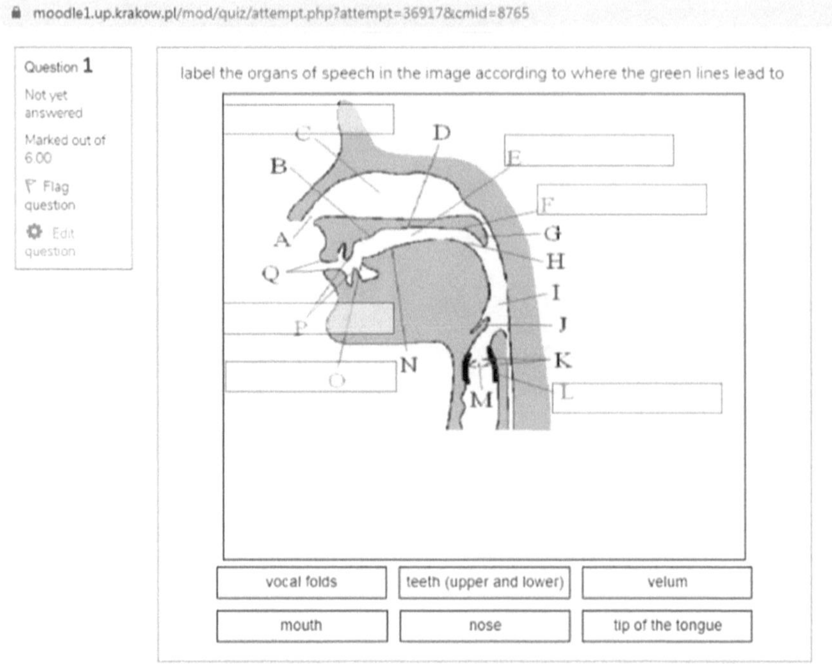

Figure 9. Sample quiz formats.

However, one of them is based on audio material (the sentence stress survey), where students first need to listen to the sentences and then answer the questions on them.

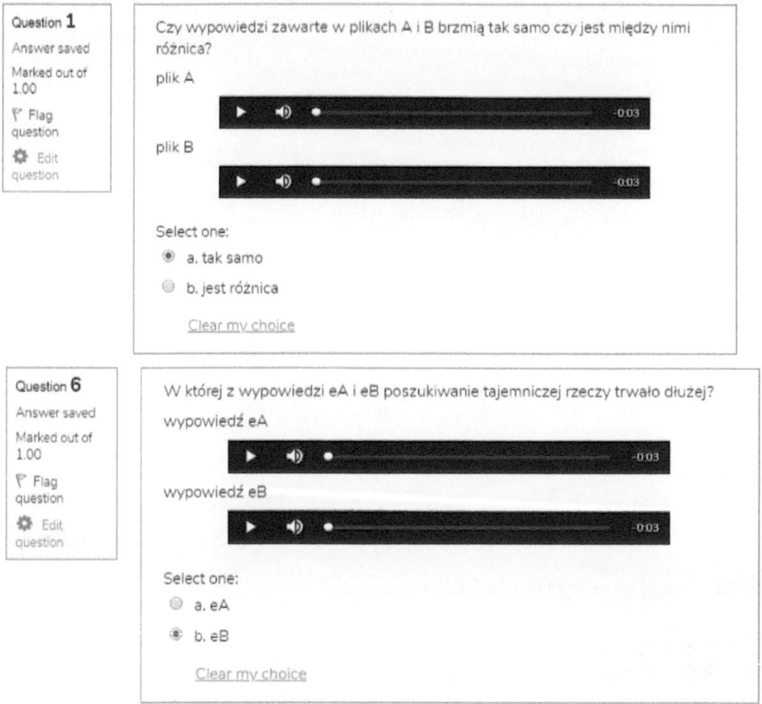

Figure 10. Samples from an audio-based quiz on sentence stress perception.

The quizzes are not simply used as assessment techniques, most of them are aimed at raising student awareness of selected aspects involved in the training. They belong to the category that could be labelled "quizzes that teach." A good example would be the Sentence Stress Survey shown above, as it requires students to reflect on their perceptive skills. Another one could be the Rhyming Words quiz, where students are to carefully match the words according to whether they are similar enough in their sound structure and actual realization. Here, additionally, they have to apply their conscious knowledge of possible interferences from their L1 (e.g. Final Obstruent Devoicing of Polish). Figure 10 shows the relevant sample.

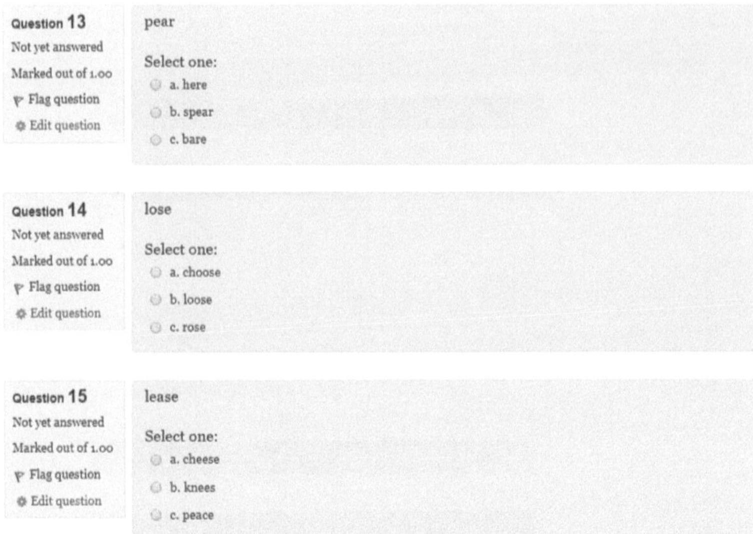

Figure 11. The Rhyming Words Quiz – a sample.

The other activity used in the online part of the Phonetics course is the format called *lesson*. It allows to transmit the relevant content in the non-overwhelming manner, at the same time, through control questions, it ensures that students invest enough attention and effort into the task. The activities designed for this course are structured so that, first of all, they contain the relevant content introduced via multitude of modes. There is text, there are images and pictures, where possible – embedded or hyperlinked videos. Since they constitute a part of a pronunciation-focused course, the text on each page is recorded, so that students can follow the text on the screen as they listen to the tutor reading it. The primary organizational principle of text transmission that is attempted to adhere to is that there cannot be too much of it in one slot/page – no scrolling should be necessary. The samples are shown in Figures 12 to 14.

3. UVULA

This is a soft, fleshy hanging tip that falls from the base of the soft palate. Have a look at the picture below.

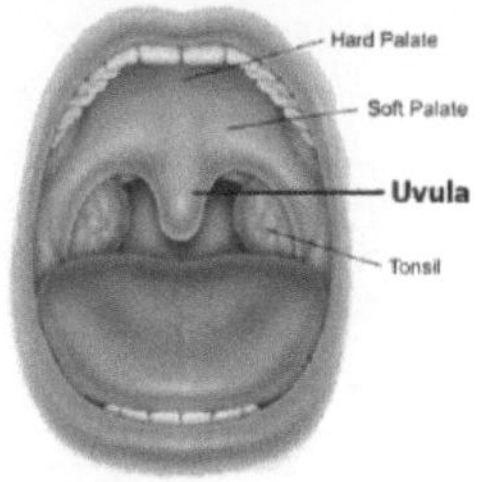

It is not directly involved in the articulation of English sounds (although it is used by some speakers with Geordie accents, i.e. from the North East of England). It is used in French for producing the French 'r' (a difficult sound for English speakers to produce when they learr French). Or the impediment (some say aristocratic) version of our Polish "czarna krowa w kropki bordo gryzła trawę kręcąc mordą".

Question: Decide which of the pairs given below produces a true equation.

- velum raised = nasal sounds
- velum lowered = oral sounds
- velum raised = oral and nasal sounds
- velum lowered = nasal sounds

Figure 12. Sample lesson pages: Text plus image.

CONSONANTS: descritpion and classification

Preview | Edit | Reports | Grade essays

> Consonants are typically described in terms of three parameters, those of VOICE and of PLACE and MANNER OF ARTICULATION.
> **VOICING**
•answers the question : are the vocal folds vibrating?
> **PLACE OF ARTICULATION**
•answers the question: where in the vocal tract is the sound made?
> **MANNER OF ARTICULATION**
•answers the question: how is the sound made?
To see the approximation as to how these parameters work, consult the University of Iowa Phonetics page
Question: *Every consonant must specified for place and manner, but voicing is accidental. TRUE or FALSE?*

- False.
- True

Figure 13. Sample lesson pages: Text plus external resource.

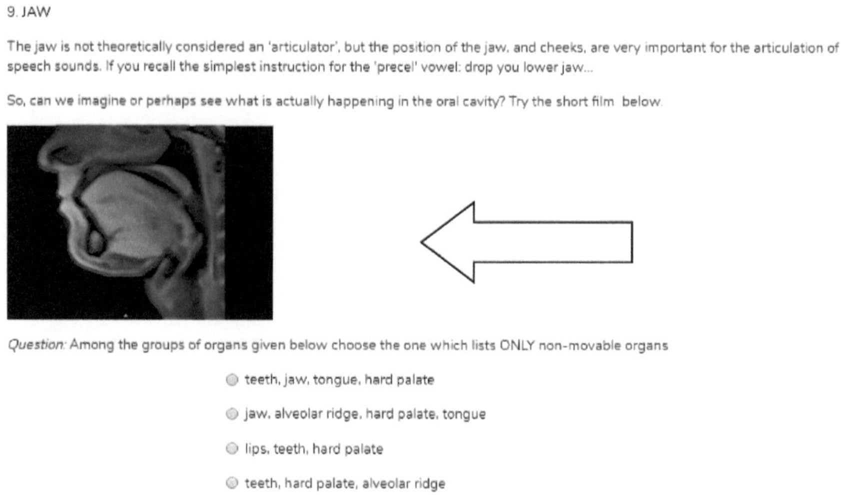

Figure 14. Sample lesson pages: Text plus video clip

In a way, a lot in terms of text, colour, image and the like is packed into the single lesson page. The approach taken here is that by doing so we cater for the different needs and learning modes of the students. Also, such polysensory presentation is more likely to reach the student and to leave a mark in their cognitive capacity.

The feedback in both types of activity is immediate: students can see the rate of good to bad responses, they may be shown the good response, they may be given extra information as to why the selected option/answer given is appropriate, or the feedback may contain a hint as to where to go to look for confirmation/good answer. The possibilities are illustrated in Figure 15, they come from quizzes and lessons.

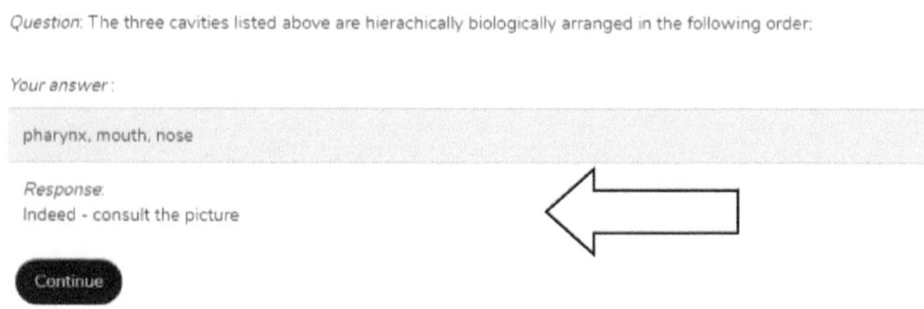

Figure 15. Samples of feedback to quizzes and lessons.

3.3. Discussion

The online part of English Phonetics course presented above constitutes approximately 30 to 35 % of the whole course, which is an outcome of mixing two different learning environments, the conventional and the digital. The view is that it thus optimizes the conditions for learning, making it more efficient. At its core it attempts to offer customized instruction based on different learning styles and needs of students. It provides continuous, unrestricted as to time and space, access to the materials and aids, it promotes conscious learning and learner autonomy in a wide sense.

The formulas applied have been designed with reference to the criteria of appropriateness to learning objectives, quality and accuracy, practicality of use and cost (Yoshida 2018). Activities such as lessons, quizzes, assignments, in their varied shapes, are prepared with those criteria in mind. Examples of the above follow in the course of the discussion. Additionally, the LMS of Moodle offers a very structured approach to course management, efficient in controlling the content and the timing of learning tools and materials. The lessons and quizzes are strictly time-controlled, for instance, and are only open to students at designated times. Serving the purpose of learning, not simply testing, multiple trials are allowed. Some of them are made available during revision time.

It has been claimed that a platform like Moodle is ideal for content-based classes (Nozawa 2011), which this one is not, at least not in its entirety. However, by using it to organize and present the course content that lends itself to such a formula, the curriculum can be strictly controlled, so that different groups of students working with different teachers get the same knowledge and practice. In other words, topics are covered to the same pattern, in the same sequence and using the same set of online and non-online materials. In the design applied here, in-class participation is one of the constituent elements of active learning, which involves cognitive activities which allow students to clarify, question, consolidate and appropriate new knowledge (Huang et al. 2019). For example, when the flipped classroom approach to sound classification topic is followed, the in-class discussions and extra activities to be done serve the purpose of first making sure that sufficient online learning has taken place and then to clarify and ultimately consolidate the unclear elements. The ICT component provides the conditions where learning occurs in the interaction between the student and the learning environment, via the technological tools and materials prepared by the instructors. In this course, for instance, students do not only somewhat passively follow a form of e-lecture, they must do so attentively to be able to move on smoothly and to be prepared either for the follow-up quiz-like activity or for in-class practice. By providing structured and timed activities we expand the subject competence and develop their tech-savvyness. Here learning becomes an interpretative process, aiming at understanding of the reality behind the sound structure of the language, thus leading to general better performance. A good example here would be incorporating video-clips unrelated primarily to phonetic matters, but actually focusing more on anatomical details (see Figures 3, 8 and 13). Students have to decode, with the help of the instructor, what these mean for their own articulation and actual performance.

The fact that the platform is used not only or even not primarily for assessment is of significance too. It must be added, though, that students rather quickly realize that such activities as are provided actually prepare them for both formative and summative evaluation. That is extended as more tasks (lessons, quizzes) are done.

Quizzes within Moodle can offer insight into how students are performing in certain topics. They can also be used to provide additional practice of aspects that appear in a regular class, both conventional and online, in our case, for example, transcription symbols, organs of speech, places and manners of articulation, homophones, or even sentence stress meaning recognition. Such information could be used to determine a student's understanding of a topic and the degree of declarative knowledge. Online quizzes offer considerably more flexibility than more traditional paper-based mid-semester tests. The course follows a module-like organization anyway, therefore any number and arrangement of quizzes can be created, at least partly in place of a mid-semester series of written tests. Figure 9 shows an example of a transcription quiz, where students need to identify the correct representation (and at the same time the correct pronunciation) of selected words. Those words have all been practiced through in-class choral and individual repetition. Students have also taken classroom-based pen-and-paper tests assessing the extent of word spoken form retention. Online test verifies that knowledge in a different manner. Students can participate in quizzes 24/7. It is anyway easier to arrange early or late online quizzes (Neill 2018). Students are permitted to see responses and answers immediately after submission, thus receiving feedback nearly instantly (see Figure 15). A benefit of using quizzes is that they can be set to be a onetime only or a replayable task, resulting in the ability for students to retake the quiz in order to progress. Thus, they may and frequently do act as supplementary presentation, practice and revision.

The lessons are particularly valuable in that they attempt to work towards multi-channelled and holistic learning experience. In the ones that deal with speech production mechanisms, for instance (see Figures 12 & 14), the mouth and the body positions, the movement of articulatory muscles, the presence or the absence of voicing airflow are presented meaningfully and clearly through text, image and sound. Thus, by manipulating speech signal the phonological awareness of the sounds in words is improved. The combination of training in visual and auditory functions enhances understanding and accelerates content retention, ultimately improving recall of the programme material, as evidenced in the summative test and exam evaluation. Thus, the human needs and instructional design meet to the effect of optimizing learning.

Many of the resources serve as additional reference bank for students after their regular face-to-face classes. In that way students can fix the information already received in regular classes, providing the same/similar content in a different format. These supplementary actions concentrate mostly on sound-symbol relationship,[9] the discrimination of syllable divisions, the prosody (intonation, stress, loudness, pitch level, juncture, speaking rate). These are presented by a variety of speakers (and, sometimes, accents), can be further analysed and accommodated. Such noticing tasks may require a certain level of metalinguistic awareness, especially when sound properties of English are compared to those of Polish. Meticulous listening to details of various recordings raises the student's awareness of specific details to be further practices and developed. Some of these make have an additional effect of interest raisers. The indirect evidence for that comes from the fact that one of the websites shown in Figure 7 (the ED-ending pronunciation tips) was actually suggested by students in class during the scheduled practice of this element.

In addition, students' willingness to learn and their learning effectiveness can be enhanced. Integrating information technology into teaching makes sense in this group because this is the area where they feel comfortable and at home. Students' learning effectiveness in higher education course can be enhanced as a result due to being motivated by immediate enjoyment and the effect of perceived success story. The team spirit is developed, too.

Admittedly, no formal research into the students' attitude and effectiveness of their learning has been done. However, external evaluation carried by the institution at the end of each semester in the form of anonymous student surveys have signalled participants' satisfaction with the course design, the

9 For instance, https://www.englishclub.com/pronunciation/phonemic-chart-ia.htm; http://www.onestopenglish.com/skills/pronunciation/phonemic-chart-and-app/interactive-phonemic-chart-british-english/.

instructional methods and the level of teacher and resultant learner competence. What has been researched (Buczek-Zawiła 2019) are the various forms of assessment that the course incorporates, both in-class and online. Here the students reported clear preference for intra-semester Moodle-organized tests, underlining their value in terms of testee-comfort, personal security, stress decrease and sustaining attention and focus. In recent years, the teachers also noted overall better test results where the tested matter concerned the material presented online, practiced in the classroom, then first quizzed online and finally, as a form of summative assessment, taken in the pen-and-paper format. The growth has been estimated to be significant, from the 34.7 % of failed attempts in 2016, to 18.7 % in 2019.

The positive influence of this hybrid mode of instruction has also become evident when the level of declarative knowledge retention is taken into consideration. The metacompetence acquired in the phonetics course is further worked on and drawn from in subsequent classes that focus on contrasting the English (L2) and the Polish (L1) grammatical systems, including at the phonological level. It thus contributes to efficient and high-quality achievement in personal and formal learning.

All this, even if indirectly, shows that at least in the case of this particular course the blended learning formula works.

4. Conclusion

The course described in this chapter has been running for several years in the formula presented above. The intra-semester results and the degree of declarative knowledge retention evident in class participation at a later stages of degree studies show that in this particular instance the *blended learning* form of instruction works. Students, to varying degrees of necessity, work independently and efficiently according to their specific needs and personal preferences, advancing in their studies. The online component allows them to do so independently of location and time. As explicitly stated by Garrison (2011: 5) "communication technologies, with their multiple media […] and their capacity to extend interaction over time and distance, are transforming teaching and learning."

This is not to say that the course cannot or should not be updated and improved. With new technological advances one can easily envisage making it more interactive than it is now. As it stands, the students now act mostly as consumers of what modern technology has prepared for them. They can become more active contributors. To give one example, as of the present students recordings are now sent to the teacher via email. That necessitates downloading and storing them, then sending back feedback to students. This can be amended by training them to upload sound recordings to the designated Moodle location. Teachers comments and/or recorded/written feedback are also stored there. The reason why this has not been implemented yet is that the course is an ongoing project, constantly being improved. The interactivity of the online portion of the course can also be extended by making students co-authors of some topics. It can easily be envisaged that they build a sort of glossary of trap words they come across in their studies, or a resource bank of instructional video clips. It would be the instructors' task to oversee such practices to the effect that they are meaningful and not simply attractive. Since the students are in the early stages of their academic careers, so far it has been deemed reasonable not to overwhelm them with the amount of technology-based work, especially in an essentially a very performance-oriented subject.

Learning performance will naturally be affected by actual teaching, course design, learning styles and multifarious other factors. The course outlined in this chapter, combining the focus on content delivery with the care on students' learning enhanced by ICT within the blended-learning formula, is believed to contribute to promoting students deep learning attitudes and quality-oriented education.

References

Argyros, I. (2012). Aspects of the holistic approach in teaching. In N. Sharafutdinova (Ed.), *Modern Technologies of Teaching Foreign Languages. Selected Papers from the International Scientific Conference.* (pp. 27–31), Ulyanovsk. Ulyanovsk: UISTU.

Barriuso, T.A. & Hayes-Harb, R. (2018). High Variability Phonetic Training as a Bridge From Research to Practice. *The CATESOL Journal*, *30.1*, 177–194.

Bataineh, R. & Mayyas, M. (2017). The utility of blended learning in EFL reading and grammar: A case for moodle. *Teaching English with Technology*, *17*, 35–49.

Buczek-Zawiła, A. (2019). Catering to assessment needs of students of English – CALL to the rescue?. Paper presented at the PL-CALL 2019 Conference, Kraków, Poland, May 30–31, 2019.

Eskenazi, M. (2009). An overview of spoken language technology for education. *Speech Communication*, *51*, 832–844.

Garrison, D. R. (2011). *E-learning in the 21st Century.* London: Routledge.

Gilakjani, A. P. (2016). English Pronunciation Instruction: A Literature Review. *International Journal of Research in English Education*, *1*(1), 1–6.

Gilakjani, A. P. & Sabouri, N. B. (2017). Advantages of Using Computer in teaching English Pronunciation. *International Journal of Research in English Education*, *2*, 78–85.

Harper, A. G. (2004) CALL-based pronunciation exercises and their effectiveness for beginning ESL learners. Proceedings of CLaSIC.

Hsieh, P., & Ji, C. (2013). The effects of computer-mediated communication by a course management system (Moodle) on English reading achievement and perceptions. Retrieved 10 April 2020 from www.atlantis-press.com/php/download_paper.php?id=8820.

Huang, Y-T., Lee, T-R. & Jiang, Y-J. (2019). The effect of teaching innovation on learning effectiveness among the students of Taiwan and Mainland China Universities. *Journal of Synergy and Research*, *7*, 111–121. DOI: http://dx.doi.org/10.17951/ijsr.2018.7.0.111-121.

Krajka, J. (2006). Web-based pronunciation teaching. *The Teacher*, *6*(40), 7–14.

Lesiak-Bielawska, E. D. (2012). The impact of blended learning on teaching English for Vocational Purposes. *Glottodidactica*, *XXXIX*, 47–56.

Levis, J. M. (2007). Computer technology in teaching and researching pronunciation, *Annual Review of Applied Linguistics*, *27*, 184–202.

Mańkowska, A., Kłoczowska, M. & Nowacka, M. (2017). *How Much Wood Would a Woodchuck Chuck. Podręcznik do nauki wymowy języka angielskiego.* Rzeszów: Wydawnictwo Wyższej Szkoły Informatyki i Zarządzania.

Mokwa-Tarnowska, I. (2015). *E-learning i blended learning w nauczaniu akademickim. Zagadnienia metodyczne*, Gdańsk: Wydawnictwo Politechniki Gdańskiej.

Neill, J. (2018, May 2). Online Quizzes and Exams with Moodle. Wikiversity. Retrieved September 9, 2019, from https://en.wikiversity.org/w/index.php?title=User:Jtneill/Teaching/Online_Quizzes_and_Exams_with_Moodle&oldid=1862062.

Nozawa, K. (2011). To moodle or not to moodle: Can it be an ideal e-learning environment?. *Political Science*, *18.3*, 289–312.

O'Brien, M., Derwing, T. M., Cucchiarini, C., Hardison, D. M., Mixdorff, H., Thomson, R. I., Strik, H., Levis, J. M., Munro, M. J, Foote, J. A., & Levis, G. (2018). Directions for the future of technology in pronunciation research and teaching. *Journal of Second Language Pronunciation*, *4*, 182–207. doi: 10.1075/jslp.17001.obr.

Plebańska, M & Kula, I. (2011). *E-learning: treści, narzędzia, praktyka*, Warszawa: ALMAMER Szkoła Wyższa.

Ponsonby, M. (1988). *How Now Brown Cow?*. New York: Phoenix ELT.

Smyrnowa-Trybulska, E. (2018). *Technologie Informacyjno-komunikacyjne i e-learning we współczesnej edukacji*, Katowice: Wydawnictwo Uniwersytetu Śląskiego.

Sobkowiak, W. (2005). Pronunciation in EFL CALL. *Teaching English with Technology*, *5*(1), 1–20.

Sun, L. (2014). Investigating the effectiveness of Moodle-based blended learning in a college English course. *International Journal of Information Technology and Management*, *13*(1), 83–94.

Tsai, Y., & Talley, P. (2014). The effect of a course management system (CMS)-supported strategy instruction on EFL reading comprehension and strategy use. *Computer Assisted Language Learning*, *27*(5), 422–438.

Turula, A. (2018). *E-learning akademicki. Perspektywa humanistyczna.* Kraków: Wydawnictwo Naukowe Uniwersytetu Pedagogicznego.

Wrembel, M. (2005). Metacompetence-oriented model of phonological acquisition: implications for the teaching and learning of second language pronunciation. *UCL, Volume Proceedings of the Phonetics Teaching and Learning Conference PTLC2005* (CD edition), London, 1–4.

Wu, W. (2008). The application of Moodle on an EFL collegiate writing environment. *Journal of Education and Foreign Languages and Literature*, 7(1), 45–56.

Yoshida, M.T. (2018). Choosing Technology Tools to Meet Pronunciation Teaching and Learning Goals. *The CATESOL Journal*, *30.1*, 195–212.

Online sources

https://anglistyka.up.krakow.pl/karty-kursow/

https://moodle1.up.krakow.pl/course/view.php?id=191

http://nf2.up.krakow.pl/course/view.php?id=24

https://www.englishclub.com/pronunciation/phonemic-chart-ia.htm;

http://www.onestopenglish.com/skills/pronunciation/phonemic-chart-and-app/interactive-phonemic-chart-british-english/

Anna Ciechanowska

Rzeszów, Poland

The assessment of language and culture competence in translation instruction: action research

Abstract: The author attempts to assess whether undergraduate English Studies students at PWSTE in Jarosław are equipped with language and culture competence, the key element of translation competence, so that they are ready to meet the demands of the competitive digital economy. In order to determine the students' linguistic knowledge and skills, the author relied on action research. The study is mainly based on the description and the analysis of linguistic mistakes made by the students and possible reasons which may have led to the problems the participants faced while performing translation tasks. An analysis of the data is carried out in order to evaluate qualitatively and quantitatively the interventions introduced in the course of instruction. The course of instruction itself is founded and developed on the assumption that it should reflect the real world working conditions, and hence the students are engaged in a business-like online environment where they provide translation services and where a translated text is a commodity that undergoes various stages for which students are accountable. Authentic translation tasks are assigned to the students in a hybrid model of instruction and the participants are evaluated on the process of task completion and the service they ultimately provide.

Keywords: translation competence, language and culture competence, action research, translation instruction, terminology, calques

1. Introduction

The problem of teaching translation to undergraduate students is not as simple and straightforward as it might seem at first glance, especially due to the fact that the traditional, teacher-centred model of translation teaching, relying on a combination of translation theory learning and translation skills drills, is not enough to train students' practical translation competence that would meet the demands of the contemporary work market. It is true that translation instruction requires both academic as well as practical training, as a strong theoretical component allows students to be aware of how and why they perform a particular translating task. On the other hand, the process of developing practical skills through practical training allows students to understand and reflect upon the text with which they are dealing and to produce translated texts meeting the standards of the translation industry. Nevertheless, even the most extensive relevant theoretical background, based on developments in neighbouring disciplines, supported by practical experience, is in itself of no value if it is not planned and carried out in an appropriate way. The appropriate way is understood here as a type of instruction that allows teachers to equip their students with translation service provision competence including language and culture, translation, technology, personal and interpersonal and service provision subcompetences, ideally under conditions resembling these governing the translation industry. Nevertheless, it must be emphasized that under conditions where students are merely offered a few curses of limited duration in translation, it seems reasonable to attempt to avoid, or at least minimize potential problems, especially in the field of language and culture competence which lies at the heart of translation competence. The ability to anticipate potential mistakes and the understanding of possible reasons behind them may turn out to be a time-saving device which, if employed in an appropriate way, may increase the effectiveness of translation courses.

2. Review of literature

How should translation training be organized in order to fulfil the need in well-qualified specialists in the area of translation? This particular question has been asked for decades by both translation experts and enthusiasts who attempt to find a satisfying recipe for a successful translation training model. Among the authors who have contributed to the development of translator education, one finds Jääskeläinen (1993; 1999), who deals with such issues as micro and macrostrategies in translation, as well as the use of think aloud protocols in translation teaching. Another researcher, Kiraly (2000; 2013), focuses on the perception of translator competence as an emergent phenomenon and discusses a social-constructivist approach to teaching translation. In the context of organizing translation training, of particular importance are the achievements of the group of researchers forming PACTE (2014; 2015), who conduct long-term empirical and experimental-based research on translation competence and its acquisition in written translation. The group's main research interests are focused on such aspects of translator training as, among others, establishing competence levels in translation and the use of new technologies in translation research. The issue of translation and translation instruction lies at the centre of attention of the members of The European Master's in Translation (henceforth: the

EMT) which is a partnership project incorporating the Directorate-General for Translation (DGT) of the European Commission and a number of universities from Europe. The core of the EMT programmes is defined by six professional competences that translation students should acquire. Another researcher, Pym (2003), attempts to find a balance between the extended needs which the work market creates in an electronic age and a minimalist concept of translation competence. The author argues that translation competence should by no means be perceived as an expanded multicomponent model, but rather as a problem-solving process that requires generalization and selection. Another significant difference, in comparison to the concepts developed by, for example, PACTE (2014; 2015) and the EMT (2017) lies in the fact that the minimalist approach clearly differentiates between language learning and translator training. Piotrowska (2013) argues that action research is a promising method in translation training, while Dybiec-Gajer (2013) deals with such issues as, for example, the assessment of the quality of translation in translation training. This is also the subject of research of Albir (2015), who discusses the process of the acquisition of translation competence and the difficulties of assessment in translation instruction. González Davies (2004) underlines the importance of the undergraduate level in translation training and the role of authentic practice in developing translation competence, which is also echoed in the work by Kelly (2005), who offers practical guidance to teaching translation to language teachers, professional translators and graduates in translation.

A universal solution to the problem of teaching translation is, arguably, impossible to find, even though there are several elements which are present in the majority of propositions regarding translation instruction. PACTE (2014; 2015), the EMT (2017) and Kiraly (2013) unequivocally state that successful translation training that would meet the needs of the contemporary translation market does not merely involve developing and cultivating language skills and the ability to use the expertise necessary to translate. It also requires preparing future translators to work in the complex circumstances of the globalized economy, where a translator is equipped not only with excellent communicative skills but also with cross-cultural and sociolinguistic awareness. Also required is technological competence, coupled with generic skills, so called *soft skills*, which enhance students' adaptability and employability. There are, however, those who argue that aspiring to such an extensive range of skills may lead translation teachers to lose sight of the aims of translation instruction. For example, as firmly stated by Pym (2003), translation instruction should not be preoccupied with technological competence as it is not the prime purpose of teaching translation.

3. Research

3.1. Research aim

The aim of the research conducted here is to determine whether assessed undergraduate students are equipped with the language and culture competence that would let them provide reliable and competitive translation of authentic technical texts, using Computer-Assisted Translation (CAT) tools in a business-like environment. The research serves as a reflective lens through which the author wants to observe some aspects of translation training and identify potential problems of translation instruction in authentic contexts. Special attention is paid to the level of linguistic knowledge and skills the participants possess, as proficient language command in both source and target languages is the starting point in any translator training programme. The author will endeavour to provide some solutions for various problems that may arise.

In order to address the challenge of assessing linguistic knowledge and skills of students and, at the same time, improving the quality of translation teaching, the following research questions have been asked: *What linguistic mistakes do the students make most frequently? Why do they make them? What may be done to increase the students' linguistic knowledge and skills?*

3.2. Research participants

The author presents the results and findings of action research carried out among the 3rd Year undergraduate English majors of State Higher School of Technology and Economics in Jarosław (Państwowa Wyższa Szkoła Techniczno-Ekonomiczna/PWSTE) who took various courses in practical translation and IT in translation, which were based on the assumption that they should reflect real work experience. Prior to the research, the students participated in a language competence test which was retrieved online. The participants' grammar, vocabulary and reading comprehension were evaluated. On completion of the test, the students were sent information about their approximate current English competence level on a CEFR scale from A1 to C2. It can be inferred from the results that 60 % of all the students who took the test are B2 learners of English, capable of understanding the most important ideas of demanding texts on both concrete and abstract topics. They can interact with native speakers with ease and create clear texts on different subjects. 11.32 % of the students are intermediate learners of English (B1), who can understand the main points of received information. They can produce simple connected texts on familiar topics, such as events, experiences and ambitions, as well as briefly give reasons and explanations for feelings and opinions. 20.79 % of the students are pre-advanced learners of English (C1). They can distinguish a wide spectrum of complex contexts and hidden meanings. They are also able to take part fluently and spontaneously in social, academic and professional contexts without seeking words and expressions. Lastly, the remaining 7.89 % of the students who took the language ability test are A2 students who are able to communicate basic information about familiar topics and routines. Moreover, they can describe aspects of their background, close environment and matters of immediate need. Based on some informal observations made during various translation courses which were offered to students before the research, as well as a survey conducted among the students of PWSTE at the beginning of the academic year,[1] one may conclude that they feel unprepared to offer their translation services in the context of the contemporary industry market. They emphasize that they face difficulties selecting appropriate strategies, looking for specialized terminology, dealing with stylistic properties of texts, both in the source and target languages. The students also admit that they have problems using certain CAT tools, organizing their time, group work and workplace autonomy.

3.3. The study: research design and data analysis techniques

To answer the research questions, the author decided to implement an action research project, a promising research paradigm with the potential to improve translation instruction (Piotrowska 2013). Action research is defined by Wallace (1987: 105) as:

> …the process through which teachers collaborate in evaluating their practices jointly; raising awareness of their personal theory; articulate a shared conception of values; try out new strategies to render the views expressed in their practice more consistent with the educational values they espouse; record their work in a form which is readily available and understandable to other teachers; and thus develop a shared theory of teaching by researching practice.

---

1 The survey is not a part of the research discussed here *per se*. It is conducted each year as a part of the quality assessment procedure in PWSTE and it addresses various aspects, for example, apprenticeship programmes, ECTS points, exchange programmes and the quality of courses offered to the students. The analysis of the results of the survey are presented to the students and discussed in order to improve the quality of education in the institution. The survey revealed that the translation instruction offered to the students requires profound re-evaluation and significant modifications.

Action research is of particular value in the case of translation teaching as it allows both teachers and students to study various problems systematically and to introduce certain interventions into the model of instruction if necessary (O'Brien 2001). As suggested by Kemmis and Wilkinson (1998), action research is a cyclical process, divided into several steps, involving planning, the implementation of various activities which are systematically observed by the instructor and the students themselves, and the observations, which are then individually and collaboratively reflected upon. Critical reflection may lead to further intervention which opens a new cycle (Winter and Munn-Giddings 2001). The new cycle is understood as an altered model of instruction and the changes implemented result from the observations and reflections following the previous cycle. The possibility of introducing various alterations systematically is the element of action research which clearly shows that its intention is to make things better than before the change. Moreover, apart from being highly beneficial for student learning experience and their academic performance, action research forces teachers to systematically analyse their research methods and expertise as it may challenge already existing beliefs, theories and concepts (Wahlstrom and Ponte 2005). It also opens new perspectives of professional development as it requires constantly enhancing the quality of teaching. Finally, among other advantages of action research, one also finds that it helps teachers to understand how practical activities are socially construed and mediated, thus reducing the gap existing between theory and practice in learning and teaching, referred to by Carr and Kemmis (1986) as *praxis*.

The action research project described in this chapter was conducted during two separate, yet related courses: IT in Translation and Technical Translation. The researcher concentrated, among others, on such aspects as employing CAT tools in translation and the development of language-specific knowledge and skills being a prerequisite for advanced translation.

As mentioned previously, the instruction itself was founded and developed on the assumption that it should reflect the real world conditions of working as much as possible. One good way to familiarize students with the translation industry is through task-based learning, involving authentic practice. Authentic practice, which is an approach advocated by many researchers, (e.g. Kiraly 2000; 2005; González Davies 2004; Kelly 2005), leads instructors to require their students to work on real translation texts. This, in turn, allows them to work in a setting well-tailored to developing not only disciplinary-specific competences but also such general competences as working in a team, autonomously or employing information and communication technology (ICT).The practical translation tasks were based on explorations of a variety of texts with different genres. The texts represented a graded (from the easiest to the most demanding) levels of difficulty and reflected the author's both hands-on experience in translating texts as well theoretical knowledge of the area.

The instruction in this action research project involved 2 cycles, divided into several steps, followed by observation and reflection stages. The observation and reflection stages were based on such research tools as: observations conducted by the instructor during the course of technical translation, translation reports (commented translation)[2] submitted by the students after each task, translation tasks and performance tests. The assessment for this study was based on both quantitative and qualitative data, which were analysed in order to understand the problem of this study and to determine if the interventions introduced were effective in increasing academic performance and student engagement in the classroom. The action research process incorporated traditional outcome assessment, where students produce some end products (translation tasks, tests, etc.) and students' perspectives of the impact the learning activity had on the learning process (translation reports), coupled with the observation conducted by the instructor.

The evaluation of the process involved multiple perspectives, however, in the present chapter the author focuses on the perspective related to the students' language-specific knowledge and skills. The analysis in this particular area allows the determination of what errors students make most frequently and why they make them. This then may show whether or not the students possess the basis for advanced translation competence.

Cycle 1 opened the action research procedure and it was divided into three steps. Step 1 was devoted to the introduction of translation theory, the element which received only fragmentary treatment due to limited time and the fact that the students are oriented towards practical tasks rather than theory. Step 2 involved the introduction of a performance test which had been chosen as one of the research tools. The latter allows the assessment of the ability to perform particular tasks, usually associated with job or study requirements (Cronbach and Meehl 1955). The test consisted of 10 short fragments to translate from Polish into English and the other way round. It involved portions written mostly in technical English. The results of the test were analysed, taking into account

2 Translation reports, according to Albir (2015), are the source of information on the process followed by students in the course of translation, the problems faced, and the documentary resources used. They make students aware of the process of translation helping them reflect on their learning process and monitor its development.

such aspects as the level of language skills, especially the use of collocations and specialized terminology. Step 3 was devoted to the implementation of task-based learning combined with collaborative learning. The first task assigned to the students required the translation of a technical text, being a description of a local watchtower. They were given similar texts to reflect on before the actual translation process, along with the glossary of technical vocabulary related to the area of architecture and construction.[3] Students were instructed to organize their group work themselves. They were free to use any CAT tools. Collaborative translation revision and correction followed after tasks completion.

After the completion of the task, the observation and reflection stages of the action research followed, which resulted in the introduction of some textual changes. The students were given individual tasks to verify how successful they are working autonomously. This particular step required the translation of short texts of technical character and it opened cycle 2. Step 2 involved task-based learning in groups again. The students were instructed to provide a translation of an instruction manual of a spin bike and RS TECHNOLOGY[4] advertising materials. In this cycle of the action research they were not given any similar texts by the instructor, instead, they were asked to find and analyse similar texts on their own out of class. As with the task assigned in cycle 1, they were instructed to organize their group work themselves and they were free to use any CAT tools. Again, translation revision and translation correction followed the completion of the tasks. The last step of cycle 2 involved the implementation of the final performance test. The observation phase in cycle 2 was based on the research tools employed in cycle 1.

3.4. Data analysis: linguistic stance

The data subject to the analysis include various types of linguistic mistakes the assessed students made as well as their observations and comments included in translation reports. Conclusions regarding the frequency and possible roots of the mistakes may help us to answer the question whether or not the

---

3 This particular step has been made to teach the students to conduct the analysis of parallel source and target language texts (that is texts from the same genre and subject area).

4 RS TECHNOLOGY is a company having its manufacturing facilities and headquarters in Gniewczyna Tryniecka. The company produces containers, storage banks, filter pressure tanks, pasteurizing and thermal treatment devices and electrical installations.

students possess the basis for advanced translation from the point of view of the level of their linguistic knowledge and skills. This can be verified through translation tasks, performance tests, observing the students while performing delegated tasks during technical translation courses and translation reports submitted by the students after each task. The mistakes selected for the analysis were taken from translation tasks and performance tests, and their choice was based on their frequency and the level of difficulty in translating determined by the students themselves in their translation reports. The analysed material was divided into three categories: calques, terminology and other mistakes. The data included in translation reports and observations conducted by the instructor were in turn used in order to determine the possible reasons of the problems faced by the students.

3.4.1. Calques

The most frequently committed type of mistakes were phraseological in nature. Among various phraseological mistakes the students committed in Polish-English translation tasks we find, for example:

- *Newralgiczne odcinki tras kolejowych* translated as *sensitive parts of the railway** – which is clearly defective as *critical/sensitive sections of the railway infrastructure* is the correct equivalent. In English we should use the noun *section* to refer to the railway infrastructure, rather than the noun *part*.
- *Całkowity zakaz budowania obiektów* translated as *full prohibition of building objects** is also a mistake as the adjective *total* should have been used, and the noun *structures* instead of *objects*. The analysed mistake resulted from the use of the wrong adjective, as *full* refers to "containing as much or as many as is possible or normal," and it may be translated as *pełen/pełny*, which is a synonym of *całkowity*, which may have caused the mistake. *Total*, in turn, is used in reference with something "involving a complete and unified effort especially to achieve a desired effect" (see Merriam-Webster),[5] hence it should have been used with the noun *ban* or *prohibition*.
- *Na dwóch narożnikach dodano wieże, pozostałe dwa ścięto* is an example of the use of a wrong verb since instead of the verb *rub down*, the verb *behead** was employed, which produced a stylistically dreadful effect.

In the case of translation tasks which required the translation from English into Polish the students faced similar problems as calques were also the most frequent mistakes, for example:

---

5 The definitions available on https://www.merriam-webster.com/dictionary/full and https://www.merriam-webster.com/dictionary/total (accessed 25.04.2019).

- *Cause an eye injury* was translated as *...spowodować obrażenia oczu**, while it should have been translated as *...spowodować uraz oczu*. The noun that collocates with the noun *oczy* (eyes) in the genitive case in Polish is *uraz*, rather than *obrażenia*. *Obrażenia* go with the nouns *ciało* or *głowa*.
- *Environmental effects* was translated as *skutki na środowisko**, instead of *wpływ na środowisko*, since the preposition *na* goes with the noun *wpływ*, not *skutki*.

Indeed, based on the analysis of mistakes made by the students, carried out by means of such tools as performance tests, translation tasks, the instructor's observation and translation reports one has to agree with Hejwowski (2006), who points out that one of the most frequently made type of mistakes, especially in texts translated by inexperienced translators, is related to the problem of selecting proper collocations. Hence, neophytes tend to produce calques violating collocatability. Another type of frequent mistakes is linked to difficulties when working with appropriate style, which results in calquing violating stylistics. In the case of the students who participated in the research these were present both in the tasks which involved translating from Polish and into Polish.

From the quantitative perspective, in the texts translated from Polish into English, in both cycles, calques constituted 57 % of all the mistakes committed by the students, and the majority of calques might be classified as calques violating collocatability (72 %), while calques violating stylistics were less common as they made up 28 %. It must be emphasized, however, that their frequency decreased in the second cycle of the research, as in the first cycle 60 % of mistakes were calques, while later the number decreased to 55 %.

In the texts translated from English into Polish calques were also the most frequently made mistakes (50 %), but the frequency of calques violating stylistics (65 %) was bigger than the frequency of calques violating collocatability (35 %). Similarly as in the case of the texts which required the translation from Polish into English, the students experienced less problems with collocations and style while translating texts from English into Polish in the second cycle, as the frequency of calques decreased to 40 %.

Calques produced by the students in Polish-English translation tasks may have been caused by the implementation of a syntagmatic approach to translation, resulting in phraseological contamination, which translation reports clearly show. It is true that "creating collocations is an instinctive act in a native language" (Dzierżanowska 1988: 32), nevertheless such an approach seems to be relatively risky in the case of languages for special purposes, such as technical English. Translating collocations might cause serious problems to novice translators and students due to the fact that it depends on a variety of factors, such as different combinability of words, synonymy, polysemy and homonymy.

These are factors which force translators to be aware of the importance of the context. Hence, the phraseology competence is one of the most decisive factors in high-quality translation. The frequency of mistakes being the result of phraseological problems indicates that in the case of the assessed students, frequently, the ability to recognize a collocation in the source language, interpret it and, eventually, find an equivalent (if there is one) in the target language is not developed enough. Another problem is that a lot of students tend to resort too frequently to literal translation, which stems from the fact that they seem to perform:

> …the transformation of literal translation, which, albeit in an implicit form, at the initial stage of the translation process is present in the translator's mind. Literal translation implies the transfer of communicatively irrelevant elements of the source text, which may result in a violation of the semantic component of the target text or a shift in semantic emphasis (Lomaka 2017:234).

It must be emphasized, however, that the author does not mean the translation which is technically "correct," but the translation which closely emulates the form, order, and linguistic idiosyncrasies of its source. For example, *…which makes iron too brittle for most applications* was translated by several students as *…co sprawia, że żelazo jest zbyt szorstkie dla większości zastosowań**, where the adjective *szorstki* is defective, even though *brittle* might be translated as *szorstki*, but not in reference to *iron*. In other words, as the data from translation reports show, it is not the problem of a word for word translation, but rather semantic literalism which consists of employing the most known, general meaning of the lexical unit instead of the contextually appropriate one, which also involves the translation of phraseological units based on the individual meanings of their components.

In the case of texts translated from English into Polish the students faced similar problems. For example, when asked to provide lists of possible equivalents for collocations, the students very frequently limited their choice to the first meaning they thought of, very frequently of literal character, without paying attention to the context, phraseology and the stylistic properties of translated texts. For example, *unwanted carbon* was translated by several students as *niechciany węgiel*, instead of *zbędny węgiel*. Such an attitude to translation also triggers another problem, namely literalism of machine translation which has turned out to be the source of a significant number of mistakes the students made in both types of tasks (Polish-English and English-Polish). The data from the reports reveal that if the students looked for collocations using one of the CAT tools, they often believed it uncritically and did not verify the suggested equivalent in another source. In several translation reports we may see that … *the iron which emerges from this process* was translated by one of the tools as *żelazo, które pojawia się z tego procesu**, which may have resulted from the fact that the students blindly trusted the tool employed.

As emerges from the present study, calques – being a standard translation procedure and one of the popular direct methods of translation – should be approached with caution since if they are employed uncritically, they introduce awkward patterns from the source language models into the target language, and, as a result, they contribute to the low quality of translated texts.

3.4.2. Terminology

Difficulties with selecting proper collocations and working with appropriate style were not the only problems the students faced as they also made terminological mistakes. Quantitatively, in the case of texts which required the translation from Polish into English, terminological mistakes constituted 33 % of all the recorded mistakes, while in the translation tasks the other way round their frequency was higher (45 %). Below, the most frequent terminological mistakes made by students in Polish-English translation tasks are presented:

- *Technika Kleina* was translated as *Klein's technique*, while suggested translation is *Klein's technology.*
- *Izba mieszkalna* was translated as *dormitory*, which semantically refers to a different referent. Suggested translation is *residential room* or *dwelling room.*
- *Skład amunicji* should have been translated as *ammunition depot*, and not as *ammunition place* or *ammunition dump.*
- *Stalowe ogrodzenie* worded as *iron fence* is clearly defective as iron and steel are entirely different materials.

As far as translation tasks from English into Polish are concerned, students faced problems of similar character. Below, the most frequent terminological mistakes are provided:

- *Feet* was translated as *stopy**, while *stopki* should have been employed.
- *Multiple power board* should have been translated as *gniazdo z rozgałęziaczem*, rather than *przedłużacz.*
- *Power steering cabinets* was translated as *szafy zasilająco-sterownicze**, while *skrzynki elektryczne* is the correct equivalent.
- *Pedal cages* translated as *klatki pedałów** is defective, as it should have been translated as *paski pedałów.*

The examples presented in the foregoing clearly show that specialized translation triggers difficulties of not merely cognitive, communicative and cultural character – that is of linguistic nature – but also of terminological character. Based on the analysis of various translations that the students produced and their own observations expressed in translation reports, the author has concluded that, not infrequently, some of them were unfamiliar with lexical, terminological or phraseological units, their meanings and grammatical use or pragmatic and stylistic value in the field of technology. Moreover, as student translation reports reveal, it often happened that if a term was not recorded in the dictionary to which they resorted, they did not know whether in the target language a certain lexicalized unit, semantically and pragmatically equivalent to the one present in the source text could be found. Some students seem to have had problems deciding whether the terms found in various specialized bilingual dictionaries were suitable for their translation. Finally, if offered different alternatives, again as their translation reports show, they seem to have had problems choosing which translation equivalent should be employed. To face these challenges effectively future translators should master a number of different skills, including:

> …the technical knowledge of a particular field (cognitive competence); a deep linguistic proficiency in both the source and target languages, which includes lexical, phraseological and terminological units (linguistic competence); and a documentary competence, on information retrieval and computerised tools available, which allows him to find the information he needs easily and quickly (Pelegrín, 2004:20).

3.4.3. Other mistakes

Apart from phraseological, stylistic and terminological mistakes, students also made other types of mistakes, including grammar and punctuation. Such errors were particularly frequent in tasks requiring translation from Polish into English, where they constituted 15 % of the mistakes. *Lotnisko Kennediego* translated as *Kennedy's airport** or *The airport of Kennedy** was the mistake which, quantitatively, was made by the largest number of students; in fact almost 45 % of the students failed to translate it correctly. The equivalents offered by this group of students are clearly defective, as they are the examples of the wrong use of the possessive case, which is used to show that something belongs to someone or a type of relationship between things. The relationship rendered in *Lotnisko Kennediego* is of a different character, as the airport does not belong to JF Kennedy. The proper equivalent is simply *Kennedy airport.*

The English-Polish translation tasks were nearly devoid of grammar mistakes (5 %), but the students seem to have had some problems with punctuation. An interesting example of a grammar mistake is the translation of *War criminals* *are tried by the International Tribunal in Hague*, which – at a glance – seems to be a relatively easy sentence to translate. However, if one does not understand the meaning of the verb *to try* in the sentence and does not notice the use of the passive voice, the effect may be the sentence: *Zbrodniarze wojenni próbują być Międzynarodowym Trybunałem w Hadze**, which may be translated as: *War criminals try to be the International Tribunal in Hague.*

As observed by the instructor and the students themselves, the presence of grammar mistakes may have resulted from three main reasons. As far as Polish-English translation tasks are concerned, some mistakes may have been made because of the incorrect generalization of rules within the target language to areas where they do not apply, for example, *the airport of Kennedy**, and interference rooted in errors resulting in the transfer of grammatical or stylistic elements from the source language to the target language, which may be related to limited linguistic competence. These reasons constitute 60 % of all grammar mistakes. Another type of grammar mistakes may be classified as performance errors which occur as a result of the working of such factors as memory lapses, confusion, fatigue or carelessness. It is important to note that the last category of mistakes applies to translation tasks in both directions. In Polish-English translation tasks, these errors make up 40 % of all the grammar mistakes, while in English-Polish translation tasks performance errors were the most common grammar mistakes, as they constituted almost 100 % of all the errors.

Another observation which must be emphasized is the fact that from the quantitative perspective, the number of mistakes decreased in the second cycle, which the final performance test and tasks performed at the end of the course clearly show.

4. Conclusion and recommendations

The two objectives of the action research conducted were to assess whether the level of linguistic skills and knowledge represented by undergraduate students subject to the research is developed well enough to allow them to meet the demands of the translation market in the online economy and to determine what errors students make most frequently while performing translation tasks, coupled with an attempt to account for the reasons behind these mistakes. Based on the analysis of the final products, the observations conducted by the instructor during the performance of delegated tasks, and the students' translation reports, the author has established that students' linguistic skills and knowledge is too limited to allow them to offer high quality translation products in the complex circumstances of the globalized economy. The frequency of the mistakes, their possible reasons and gaps in other related areas, such as the use of CAT tools or specialized languages, show that translation teaching programmes, especially those limited in time, should be altered to increase the quality and to facilitate the learning process of the students. What could be done then to boost the quality of translation teaching programmes and to avoid potential problems? Before introducing courses involving specialized translation several steps could be taken:

- at least 1-semester long course in translation theory should be offered,
- students should be offered courses in ESP to reflect on their typical features, terminology and style,
- university curriculum should involve courses of Polish and English stylistics,
- practical English courses should be extended,
- the introduction of the main principles of the general theory of phraseology would also help to address problems with translating collocations.

These recommendations may help to deal with problems related – partially – to the competences included in translation competence put forward by the EMT, namely the competence that "encompasses all the general or language-specific linguistic, sociolinguistic, cultural and transcultural knowledge and skills that constitute the basis for advanced translation competence."[6] The improvement in this particular area is, however, of primary importance as language-specific knowledge and skills are the driving force behind all the other competences forming translation competence. While this study is undoubtedly limited, it sheds some light on the potential problems translation instructors may face when challenged to teach specialized translation to undergraduate students, especially having very limited time at their disposal. It can also help to determine what alterations could be introduced to improve the quality of translation instruction. Nevertheless, in order to verify the outcome of the implementation of such changes a larger-scale study is required.

References

Albir, H. (2015). The acquisition of translation competence. Competences, tasks and assessment in translator training. *Meta Translators' Journal, 60*(2), 256–280.

6 The quotation taken from https://ec.europa.eu/info/sites/info/files/emt_competence_fwk_2017_en_web.pdf (accessed 25.04.2019).

Carr, W. & Kemmis, S. (1986). *Becoming Critical: Education, Knowledge and Action Research*. London: Falmer.

Cronbach, L.J. & Meehl, P.E. (1955). Construct validity in psychological tests. *Psychological Bulletin*, *52*, 281–302.

Dybiec-Gajer, J. (2013). *Zmierzyć przekład. Z metodologii oceniania w dydaktyce przekładu pisemnego*. Kraków: Universitas.

Dzierżanowska, H. (1988). *Przekład tekstów nieliterackich*. Warszawa: Państwowe Wydawnictwo Naukowe.

European Master's in Translation (2017). Available at https://ec.europa.eu/info/resources-partners/european-masters-translation-emt/european-masters-translation-emt-explained_en.

González Davies, M. (2004). Undergraduate and postgraduate translation degrees: Aims and expectations. In K. Malmkjaer (Ed.), *Translation as an Undergraduate Degree* (pp. 67–81). Amsterdam: John Benjamins.

Göpferich, S. (2009). Towards a model of translation competence and its acquisition: The longitudinal study "TransComp." In S. Göpferich, A. L. Jakobsen & I. M. Mees (Eds.), *Behind the Mind. Methods, Models and Results in Translation Process Research. Copenhagen Studies in Language 37* (pp. 11–37). Copenhagen: Samfundslitteratur Press.

Hejwowski, K. (2006). *Kognitywno-komunikacyjna teoria przekładu*. Warszawa: Wydawnictwo Naukowe PWN.

Jääskeläinen, R. (1999). *Tapping the process. An explorative study of the cognitive and affective factors involved in translating*. Joensuu: University of Joensuu Press.

Jääskeläinen, R. (1993). Investigating translation strategies. In S. Tirkkonen-Condit & J. Laffling (Eds.), *Recent Trends in Empirical Translation Research. Studies in Languages No 28* (pp. 99–120). Joensuu: University of Joensuu Press.

Kelly, D. (2005). *A Handbook for Translator Trainers*. Manchester: St Jerome.

Kemmis, S. &Wilkinson, M. (1998) Participatory action research and the study of practice. In B. Atweh, S. Kemmis & P. Weeks (Eds.), *Action Research in Practice. Partnerships for Social Justice in Education* (pp. 21–36). London: Routledge.

Kiraly, D. (2013). Towards a view of translator competence as an emergent phenomenon: thinking outside the box(es) in translator education. In D. Kiraly, S. Hansen-Schirra & K. Maksymski (Eds.), *New Prospects and Perspectives for Educating Language Mediators* (pp. 197–224). Tübingen: Narr

Kiraly, D. (2005). Situating praxis in translator education. In: K. Károly & Á. Föris (Eds.), *NewTrends in Translation Studies — Festschrift für Kinga Klaudy* (pp. 117–138). Budapest: Akademiai Kiado.

Kiraly, D. (2000). *A Social-Constructivist Approach to Translator Education.* Manchester: St. Jerome.

Lomaka, A. (2017). Literal approach to translation: a classification and literature review. *XLinguae, 10*(4), 234–244.

O'Brien, R. (2001). An overview of the methodological approach of action research. In R. Richardson (Ed.), *Theory and Practice of Action Research* (pp. 1–18). Joao Pessoa: Universidade Federal da Paraíba.

PACTE (2015). Results of PACTE's experimental research on the acquisition of translation competence: the acquisition of declarative and procedural knowledge in translation. The dynamic translation index. *Translation Spaces*, *4*(1), 29–53.

PACTE (2014). First results of PACTE group's experimental research on translation competence acquisition: The acquisition of declarative knowledge of translation. *MonTI Special Issue*, *1*, 85–115.

Pelegrín, J. G. (2004). Prólogo. In C. Gonzalo García & V. García Yebra (Eds.), *Manual de documentación y terminología para la traducción especializada* (pp. 19–22). Madrid: Arco/Libros

Piotrowska, M. (2013). Action research in translation studies. Self-reflection in translation research training. *Między oryginałem a przekładem*, *19*(1/2), 153–169.

Pym, A. (2003). Redefining translation competence in an electronic age. In defence of a minimalist approach. *Meta Translators' Journal, (48)4*, 481–497.

Wahlstrom K. & Ponte, P. (2005). Examining teachers' beliefs through action research: Guidance and counselling/pastoral care reflected in the cross-cultural mirror. *Educational Action Research Journal, 13*(4), 543–561.

Wallace, M. (1987). A historical review of action research: Some implications for the education of teachers in their managerial role. *Journal of Education for Teaching, 13*(2), 97–115.

Winter *R. &* Munn-Giddings, C. (2001*). A Handbook for Action Research in Health and Social Care.* London: Routledge.

Online sources

https://ec.europa.eu/info/sites/info/files/emt_competence_fwk_2017_en_web.pdf.

https://www.merriam-webster.com/dictionary/full.

Natalia Góralczyk
Pedagogical University, Kraków, Poland

Teaching foreign languages to older people using new technologies from a teacher's perspective

Abstract: The objective of the research was to investigate English teachers' attitudes towards using new technologies in a foreign language classroom with older adults. The results of the study revealed that most of the participants agreed that teaching foreign languages with the use of new technologies was possible and beneficial. The participants were also asked to choose which Web 2.0 learning technologies based on Bower's typology (2016) they consider effective, which was later compared with the literature review on this topic.

Keywords: older person, Web 2.0. learning technologies, glottogeragogics

1. Introduction

The transition towards a much older population structure is increasingly recognized as a serious, worldwide concern (Eurostat 2018). Ergo, it is more probable to encounter older learners in a foreign language classroom, and so understanding the area of older adult foreign language learning should become the primary concern of researchers and practising teachers.

It is necessary here to clarify exactly what is meant by using the terms "an older person." There is a degree of uncertainty around what is meant by using the term "an older person." For the purpose of this study, it should be assumed an older person is a person aged 60 and over. It is due to the fact that the most common age limit that is said to be the beginning of old age is 60 or 65, and the age 60 and over is the one accepted by United Nations and WHO (United Nations 2017a; Zych 2007). Nevertheless, in Figure 1 in the demographic section, an older person is classified as a person aged 60 and over, which is the definition supported by OECD (2019). The other two important terms i.e. glottogeragogics and Web 2.0. learning tools are explained further in the paper.

The aim of this research project is, therefore, to try and establish what attitudes foreign language teachers have towards teaching older people using new technologies, which Web 2.0. learning tools might facilitate the learning process, and how those results compare with the literature on that topic.

The paper begins with a brief overview of demographic ageing. It then goes on to discuss the older learner, glottogeragogics, and research in the area of new technologies with the focus on Web 2.0. learning tools, and foreign language learning. Finally, the paper discusses the results of the study, along with its conclusions.

1.1. Demographic ageing

Due to the advancements in the field of medicine and technology as well as economic development, people live healthier and longer and their quality of life is better when compared to the past. But at the same time, this process poses a great challenge on multiple levels when it comes to addressing its implications (National Institute of Aging 2007). One of the implications is the increasing number of older people, and this can be observable on a global scale. The global population aged 60 years and over was 962 billion in 2017 and is expected to be 2.1. billion in 2050, which is at least twice as many. It is projected that there will be more older people than children under age 10 in 2030 and young people aged 10–24 in 2050. In Europe, older people will have become 35 % of the total European population, and in Poland, this number will be even higher because it is predicted to be 40 %. In Poland, there were 8.4 million older people (aged 60 and over) in 2015, and it is estimated to be 13.7 million in 2050 (Barbadyn 2017; United Nations 2017b). Figure 1 demonstrates the steady increase in the total population in OECD countries (OECD 2019).

One of the ways in which such increased life expectancy is dealt with is the gradual rise of the official retirement age. If people are expected to work longer in their lives in this rapidly changing reality, it consequently brings the attention to the need for continuing lifelong education (National Institute of Aging 2007; OECD 2017). But as lifelong education might be primarily connected with institutional learning, the term "lifelong learning" should be used to include the fact that learning may be intentional or not, take place in different settings, and be of "recurrent nature" in general (Jarvis 2014: 53). Lifelong learning is said to positively impact older people's quality of life and integrate important new skills into their lives, including foreign language and ICT skills (Escuder-Mollon et al. 2014).

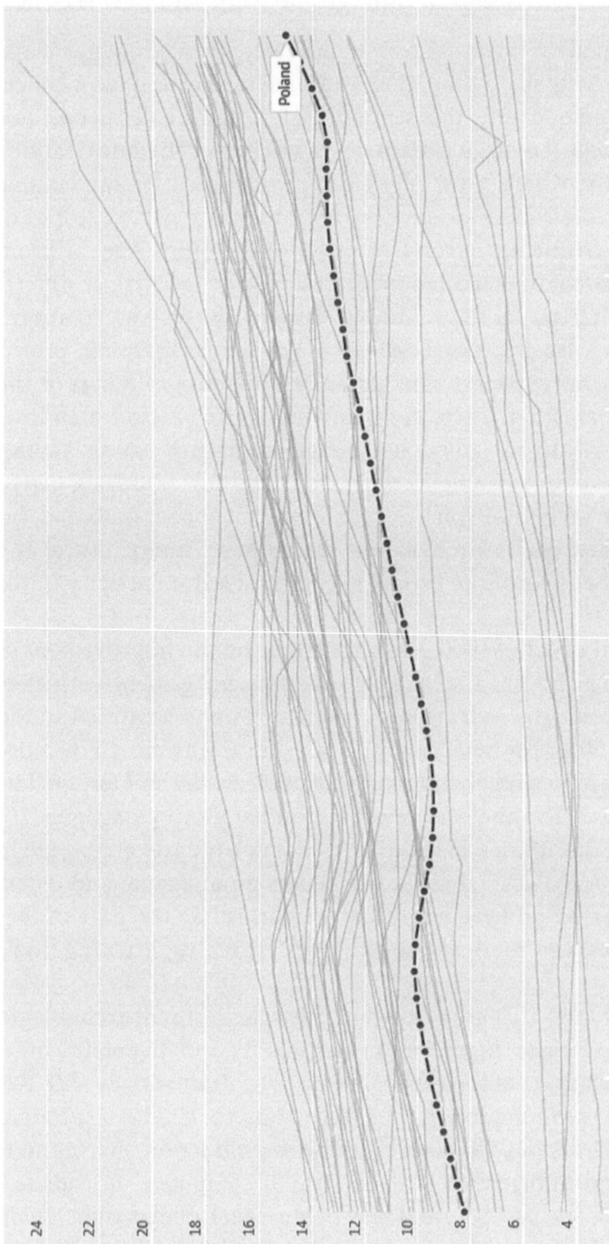

Figure 1. Population of older people (aged 65 and over) Total, % of population, 1970 – 2014 (OECD 2019).

1.2. Older learner, foreign language learning and new technologies

Having elaborated on the prognosis of older people making up a considerable proportion of the global population and lifelong learning as a concept positively influencing one's life, this section analyses how older people find themselves in a foreign language classroom as well as in the information society, more specifically: where, how, why older people learn foreign languages and what effects of such learning process are. An older person learns a foreign language most frequently at the University of the Third Age, by himself/herself, or through commercial language courses for learners at different ages. The activities that are most commonly observed in such a classroom include note-taking, discussions, clarifications of problems, listening, projects, field education, presenting papers, conducted in different groupings or this might be passive participation. There are many motivating factors standing behind older learners' willingness to pursue foreign language learning, among others, to maintain/develop my intellectual efficiency, for travelling purposes, to communicative with family, friends, or simply new people abroad, because it is necessary when one is a member of the modern, multicultural and multilingual world, because of life experience, or as a leisure activity (Jaroszewska 2013a; 2013b).

The expected effect of their learning might be the improvement of cognitive functioning and one's self-esteem, better engagement with the society, and it might mean the reduction of costs for public health (Antoniou et al. 2013; Klimova 2018; National Institute of Adult Continuing Education 2015). To research the issues revolving around older learners and foreign languages, a relatively new discipline was developed called glottogeragogics. It benefits from two other disciplines, glottodidactics which focuses on foreign language learning and geragogics, which is the pedagogy of ageing and older people. The study reported on here might be categorized as the part of the field of glottogeragogics i.e. methods, techniques, teaching/learning tools (Zych 2017).

The learning tools that are studied in this article are the technological ones. How older people place themselves in this rapidly evolving reality of technologies becoming the part of their daily lives will be dealt with as well. Nowadays, older people have to function in the information society i.e. a society in which technology and human skills enable unlimited production, sharing and shaping of e-services and information with the use of computers. It leads to changes within society, work, lifestyle, and may be the cause of exclusion (Siemieniecki

2007). More and more commercial and public services are available on the Internet. Digital exclusion will cover increasingly more aspects of life due to the development of phenomena such as the Internet of Things. Today's digital exclusion does not imply simply the lack of the necessary equipment or the Internet connection, but digital competences and motivations to benefit from ICT. For that reason, developing such competences is crucial in terms of e-inclusion (Tarkowski et al. 2015).

According to Marcinkiewicz-Wilk (2016), older people are positive towards such new reality as they perceive it as an opportunity for personal development and they understand the need to develop especially their ICT and interpersonal skills. Older people observe that thanks to being a part of the information society they can access any knowledge in a simple and quick way and keep in touch with other people. Ergo, it might be said that technologies satisfy older people's basic needs for contact and information. However, their level of digital competences is low and it decreases in digital efficiency with age on account of their skills, experience, physical ageing, not to mention other variables such as their needs, attitudes, or life situation (Tarkowski et al. 2015). Although the majority of older people in Poland do not use modern technologies, many of them express their interest in acquiring new knowledge and participate in courses and training sessions (Kuchta 2013).

1.3. Web 2.0. learning technologies

Web 2.0 technologies can be described as "openly available online technologies that allow creation, editing and sharing between (often large) groups of people via a web-browser. This definition [...] is based on the functionality of the tools rather than their implications so as to support objective selection for sampling purposes" (Bower 2016: 765). Bower's typology of Web 2.0 learning technologies hinges on structured typological analysis, not user experience, i.e. the elements within the types of the tools are very much related, but at the same time, the types of the tools are very much distinct (Given 2008). The selection criteria included: the key characteristics of the tools i.e. they are openly available and free, educationally applicable, can be used from a web browser for creating, editing and sharing purposes (Bower 2016: 769). It resulted in a typology of 37 Web 2.0 learning technologies organized into 14 larger clusters that can be seen in Figure 2.

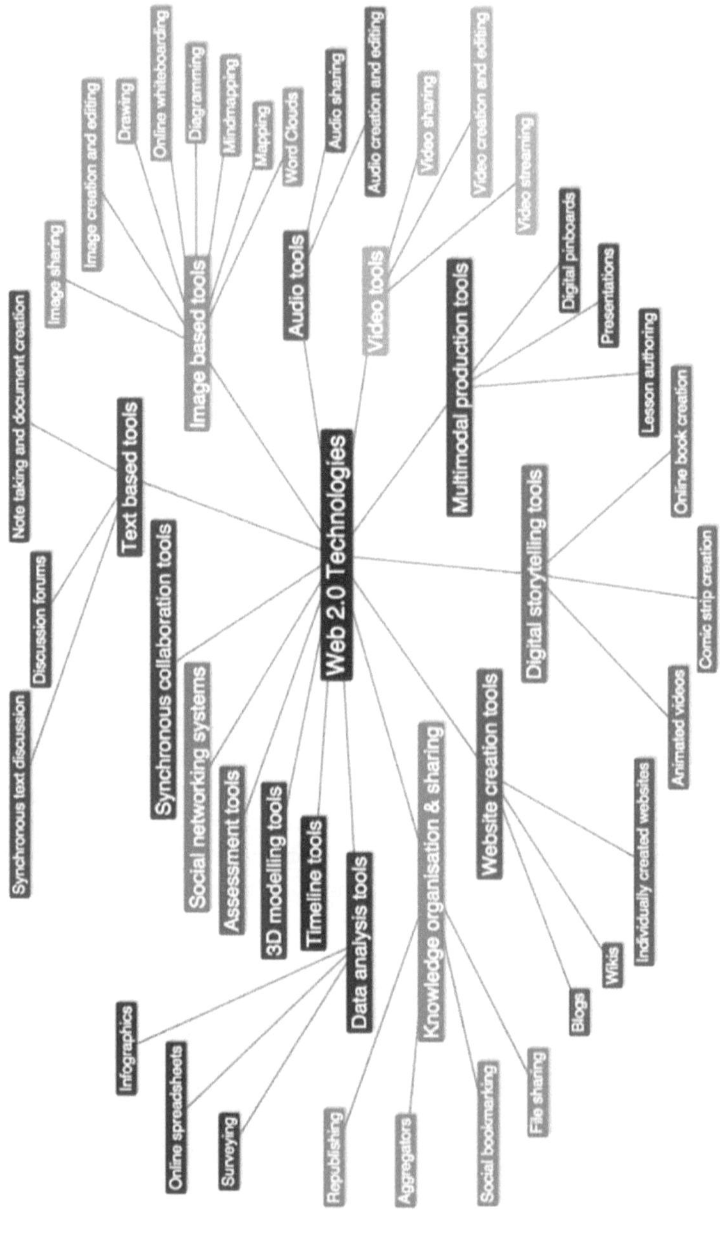

Figure 2. Typology of Web 2.0 learning technologies (Bower 2015: 2).

What Bower (2016) demonstrates is that a key factor for differentiating between given Web 2.0. tools are how information and communication are organized within them. Those tools can be used in multiple ways depending on the task and users' interaction. The number of Web 2.0. tools is growing and the use of them is fluctuating, some tools gain in popularity to the detriment of others. Finally, he expresses his goal to "aims to increase their conception of how technology can be used to engage learning, and how learners may arrive at new ways of knowing" (Bower 2016: 774).

The purpose of the present study is to elaborate on this thought in terms of if "technology can be used to engage learning" in a foreign language class with older learners and which Web 2.0 learning technologies can be utilized in classes with older foreign language learners from a teacher's perspective.

2. Review of literature

In recent years there has been a growing interest in new technologies and older learners as their users, but not much work on their potential in a foreign language classroom has been carried out. A number of studies have been conducted that investigate the role of Web 2.0. learning technologies in older people's lives. Three major benefits of their incorporation can be distinguished and are summarized in Table 1.

Table 1. The benefits of incorporating Web 2.0. learning technologies in older people's lives.

THE BENEFIT	WEB 2.0. TECHNOLOGIES
Improved social-emotional competences (socialization, preventing social isolation and loneliness)	digital storytelling tools (Hausknecht et al. 2017) social networking sites (Harley et al. 2014). synchronous collaboration tools (Blussi et al. 2018) text based tools (Harley et al. 2014). website creation tools (Wrońska 2017)
Maintained/Improved cognitive functioning	digital storytelling tools (Hausknecht et al. 2017) social networking sites (Quinn 2018) website creation tools (Wrońska 2017)
An opportunity for creative output	audio tools (O'Keeffe 2017) digital storytelling tools (Hausknecht et al. 2017) video tools (Ferreira et al. 2017) website creation tools (Wrońska 2017)

Only a few studies have been published on the topic of teaching older people foreign languages with the use of new technologies. The study conducted by Ware et. al. (2017) examined the advantages of integrating foreign language learning and technology. The main outcomes were measured with the use of questionnaires and interviews. The findings showed that the participants' cognitive levels did not change significantly but they found such integration helpful, entertaining, and stimulating to use technology in a foreign language course. This integration was facilitative especially for the participants with a more advanced level of English and ICT skills. Still, the main downside of this study is that it was connected with Web 1.0 technologies. Web 1.0. technologies are not interactive as they are mostly limited to sharing content online in comparison with Web 2.0. technologies, which enable communication and knowledge production, and so are more dynamic in nature (Choudhury 2014).

The aim of another study (Bru Ronda & Belda-Medina 2018) was to elaborate on the benefits of purposeful implementation of new technologies in a foreign language classroom. The results revealed that thanks to such combination of technology and language classes, older people master their skills, successfully deal with their anxiety, and build their self-confidence. The key problem is that older learners assessed themselves in the post-test. One question that needs to be raised concerning that measurement of outcomes is how the participants would have performed in the summative assessment done by the researcher.

To sum up, with regard to the studies that focus on those three elements i.e. older learner, foreign language learning and new technologies, it might be observed that this field of knowledge provides some promising insight, yet is not widely understood.

3. The study

3.1. Research design

The research tool was an online survey with both close-ended and open-ended questions, conducted at the turn of September and October 2018. There were 150 participants who were English Teachers, the members of a popular among Polish English Teachers "English Teachers" (facebook.com/groups/nauczycieleangielski). They were the residents of cities over 300.000 (60 %) who completed their MA studies (74 %). Their experience in foreign language teaching was usually less than 5 years or between 5 and 10 years. Their most common workplace were a language school, university or private lessons. Their experience in teaching older learners was fair (53 %), little (21 %), and good (12 %) (Góralczyk 2019).

The study tried to answer 3 research questions:

1. Is teaching a foreign language to older people possible with the use of new technologies from the teachers' perspective?
2. Which Web 2.0 learning technologies classified by Bower (2016) are considered older person foreign language learning facilitators by teachers?
3. Are the selected Web 2.0 learning technologies in accordance with the literature review in this area by teachers?

3.2. Findings

Addressing the first research question, the majority of respondents agreed or slightly agreed that teaching older adults using new technologies is possible (Figure 3).

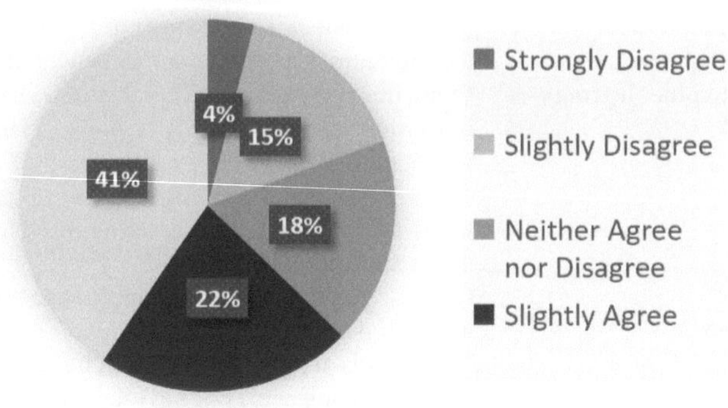

Figure 3. The participants' opinion concerning teaching foreign languages to older people with the use of new technologies.

Their justifications were divided into several categories and can be seen in the following figure (Table 2).

Table 2. The participants' justification for their opinion concerning teaching foreign languages to older people with the use of new technologies.

TYPE OF JUSTIFICATION	EXAMPLES
Opinions of respondents who teach older people and successfully implement new technologies	"I teach using new technologies, seniors like it and appreciate it. I teach beginners, hence not all digital tools are suitable." "I worked with a student about 70 years old with whom I used various technologies that proved to be very effective."
Opinions focused on new technologies	"Modern technologies aim to make the educational process more attractive and increase the pupil's chance of acquiring a foreign language. In my opinion, it gives them a universal character." "Older people use technologies more and more often." "More and more older people can use modern technologies and are interested in this. The use of modern technologies enriches lessons for people of all ages."
Opinions that took into account the need to adapt new technologies to older learners	"I believe that elders are eager to approach new technologies if they have someone who introduces them, but I do not think that the total abandonment of traditional methods (paper, books, blackboard) was good due to the habits of such people." "New technologies can improve the process of teaching people if they are well-tailored to individual needs and the level of familiarity with new technologies of a given person because they will not understand the mechanisms." "If the tools are intuitive and can be adapted to the needs of people with poor eyesight/hearing, they can be used as much as possible."
Opinions that took into account the motivating factors of older people	"A frequent motivation among older people is having a family (children, grandchildren) brought up in a different language environment, which is why learning new technologies allows to find a "common language" also in life, allows "keeping up" with younger members of the family. People in this situation will be happy to learn new tools." "New technologies accompany us every day. However, everything depends on whether older people are interested in this way of learning." "It depends on the age of the participant, his familiarity with technology and his belief that such science 'has a meaning.'"
Opinions that were generally negative	"Some people are not willing to use technology, they cannot use a computer, they are afraid of it."

As far as the answer to the second research question is concerned, the participants were supposed to choose the Web 2.0 technologies which they considered facilitating in a foreign language classroom with older learners. The results revealed that more than half of the participants consider facilitating video sharing tools (98.7 %), online book creation (83.3 %), wikis (74.7 %), presentations (71.3 %), social networking sites (69.3 %), assessment tools (65.3 %), digital pinboards (58.7 %), mindmapping (57 %), and notetaking and document creation tools (54 %) (Table 3).

Table 3. Web 2.0 learning tools that are considered facilitating older person foreign language learning from a teacher's perspective.

TEXT BASED TOOLS		Infographics, e.g. Canva	34.7 %
Synchronous text discussion, e.g. Twitter, TodaysMeet	28 %	**AUDIO TOOLS**	
Discussion forums	42.7 %	Audio sharing, e.g. Soundcloud	28 %
Notetaking and document creation, e.g. Google Docs	**54 %**	Audio creation and editing, e.g. Vocaroo	12.7 %
IMAGE BASED TOOLS		**VIDEO TOOLS**	
Image sharing, e.g. Flickr, Instagram	34 %	Video sharing, e.g. YouTube, TeacherTube	**98.7 %**
Image creation and editing, e.g. Adobe Sparks	2.7 %	Video creation and editing, e.g. Screencast-o-matic, Kizoa	12.7 %
Drawing/online whiteboarding, e.g. Google Quick Draw, Sketch.io	2 %	Video streaming, e.g. Younow	12 %
Diagramming, e.g. Draw.io	4.7 %	**MULTIMODAL PRODUCTION TOOLS**	
Mindmapping e.g. Mindomo	**57 %**	Digital pinboards, e.g. Padlet	**58.7 %**
Mapping, e.g. Google Maps	21 %	Presentations, e.g. Prezi, Google Slides	**71.3 %**
Word clouds, e.g. Wordle	32 %	Lesson authoring, e.g. Edpuzzle	24.7 %
DIGITAL STORYTELLING TOOLS		**WEBSITE ORGANIZATION AND SHARING TOOLS**	
Online book creation, e.g. Storybird	**83.3 %**	File sharing, e.g. Google Drive, Dropbox	8 %
Comic strip creation, e.g. Bitstrips	18 %	Social bookmarking, e.g. Memonic	11.3 %
Animated videos, e.g. Powtoon	18.7 %	Aggregators, e.g. Flipboard	0 %

(continued on next page)

Table 3. Continued

WEBSITE CREATION TOOLS		Republishing, e.g. Scoop.it, Pinterest	34 %
Individual website creation, e.g. Google Sites, Weebly	28 %	**OTHER TOOLS**	
Wikis, e.g. Wikia	**74.7 %**	Timeline tools, e.g. Outstory, Timetoast	2 %
Blogs, e.g. Blogger, Tumblr	38 %	3D modeling tools, e.g. Shapeshifter.io	0 %
DATA ANALYSIS TOOLS		Assessment tools, e.g. Quizlet, Socrative	**65.3 %**
Conducting surveys, e.g. Surveymonkey	33.3 %	Social networking sites, e.g. Facebook, Edmodo	**69.3 %**
Online spreadsheets, e.g. Google Sheets	3.3 %	Synchronous collaboration tools, e.g. Zoom.us, Google Hangouts	30.7 %

3.3. Discussion

The participants are rather positive towards teaching older learners foreign languages with the use of new technologies and refer in their justifications to their teaching experience and the advantages of new technologies. They also stress the need to construct the learning process in such a way that would appropriately address older learners' level of ICT skills and what motivates them to start a language course in the first place. Some respondents believe older learners are rather not motivated to develop their ICT skills so as to participate in such a language course.

The common belief is that the respondents can use effectively almost every Web 2.0 learning tool in a foreign language classroom with older learners. However, there are categories of tools that are not a popular choice among teachers, and these are data analysis tools, audio tools, website organization and sharing tools, timeline and 3D modelling tools.

When comparing the data from the study and the literature review, it transpires that there is an overlap between them. Assessment tools, social networking sites, digital storytelling tools (online book creation) and image based tools (mindmapping) are mentioned in both the study and the literature (Bru Ronda & Belda-Medina 2018; Harley et al. 2014; Repetto & Trentin 2008).

There was no research connected with video sharing, Wikis, presentations or note-taking specifically. However, there is research outlining the advantages of digital video production (Ferreira et al. 2017) and blogs (Wrońska 2017) which also fall into the categories of video and website creation tools respectively. Not to mention that older people enjoy the presentation format and taking notes during their classes (Jaroszewska 2013b), which might be connected with their learning experience i.e. traditional learning strategies and activities that are familiar forms. Perhaps if those activities were digitalized with the use of Web 2.0 learning technologies, such bridge between traditional and digital approach would increase the effectiveness of the learning process as well as their level of older people's satisfaction. Synchronous collaboration tools, text based tools, and audio tools were not chosen by the participants, although there is evidence of their benefits in connection with older learners.

4. Conclusion

More than half of the participants believe that teaching a foreign language to older people is possible with the use of new technologies, but such learning process needs adaptation to older people's motivations and needs. Many learning tools of almost every type were found to be considered to facilitate the foreign language learning process, which was mostly in accordance with the results from the literature review.

This study carried out in this specific area of research was a preliminary attempt to establish foreign language teachers' position as to what their attitude towards teaching foreign languages to older learners are and which Web 2.0 learning technologies they find facilitating.

This research has raised many questions in need of further investigation. For instance, foreign language teachers should be asked to elaborate on the ways they have used/would use such Web 2.0 learning tools. Furthermore, the effectiveness of these technologies should be researched in more detail in a foreign language classroom environment.

References

Antoniou, M., Gunasekera, G. M., & Wong, P. C. M. (2013). Foreign language training as cognitive therapy for age-related cognitive decline: a hypothesis for future research. *Neurosci. Biobehav. Rev. 37*, 2689–2698.

Barbadyn, M. (2017). *Country report – POLAND Information on Polish action on older persons – Implementation of the Madrid Plan of Action on Ageing in 2012–2016*. Warsaw: Ministry of Family, Labour and Social Policy. Retrieved from https://www.unece.org/fileadmin/DAM/pau/age/country_rpts/2017/POL-Report-EN.pdf.

Blusi, M., Nilsson, I. & Lindgren, H. (2018). Older Adults Co-Creating Meaningful Individualized Social Activities Online for Healthy Ageing. *Studies in Health Technology and Informatics. 247,* 775–779.

Bower, M. (2016). Deriving a typology of Web 2.0 learning technologies. *British Journal of Educational Technology, 47*(4), 763–777.

Bower, M. (2015). *A Typology of Web 2.0 Learning Technologies.* Retrieved from https://library.educause.edu/resources/2015/2/a-typology-of-web-20-learning-technologies.

Bru Ronda, C. & Belda-Medina, J. (2018). *Using Technology to Motivate Senior Students in Second Language (L2) Learning.* AIUTA INTERNATIONAL CONFERENCE · Standards of Education among U3as and the Intergenerational Formatio. Retrieved from https://www.researchgate.net/publication/326000098_Using_Technology_to_Motivate_Senior_Students_in_Second_Language_L2_Learning.

Choudhury, N. (2014). World Wide Web and Its Journey from Web 1.0 to Web 4.0. *International Journal of Computer Science and Information Technologies, 5*(6), 8096–8100. Retrieved from http://ijcsit.com/docs/Volume%205/vol5issue06/ijcsit20140506265.pdf.

Escuder-Mollon, P., Esteller-Curto, R., Ochoa, L. & Bardus, M. (2014). Impact on Senior Learners' Quality of Life through Lifelong Learning. *Procedia – Social and Behavioural Sciences, 131,* 510–516. Retrieved from https://www.sciencedirect.com/science/article/pii/S1877042814030675.

Eurostat. (May 2018). *Population structure and ageing.* Retrieved from https://ec.europa.eu/eurostat/statistics-explained/index.php?title=Population_structure_and_ageing&oldid=423053.

Ferreira, S. M., Sayago, S. & Blat, J. (2017). Older people's production and appropriation of digital videos: an ethnographic study. *BEHAVIOUR & INFORMATION TECHNOLOGY, 36*(6), 557–574.

Given, L. M. (2008). *The SAGE encyclopedia of qualitative research methods* (Vols. 1–0). Thousand Oaks, CA: SAGE Publications. Retrieved from http://methods.sagepub.com/reference/sage-encyc-qualitative-research-methods/n472.xml.

Góralczyk, N. (2019). Czy nauczyciele języka obcego są przygotowani do uczenia osób starszych?. *Języki Obce w Szkole, 2,* 61–65.

Harley, D., Howland, K., Harris, E. & Redlich, C. (2014). *Online communities for older users: what can we learn from local community interactions to create social sites that work for older people.* Proceedings of the 28th International BCS Human Computer Interaction Conference (HCI 2014). Southport, UK, 9–12 September 2014. Retrieved from https://pdfs.semanticscholar.org/0871/f0ac37805767a9836607c0f1a8017693d3d9.pdf.

Hausknecht, S., Vanchu-Orosco, M. & Kaufman, D. (2017). Sharing Life Stories: Design and Evaluation of a Digital Storytelling Workshop for Older Adults. In: G. Costagliola, J. Uhomoibhi, S. Zvacek & B. McLaren (Eds.), *Computers Supported Education. CSEDU 2016. Communications in Computer and Information Science, 739*. (pp. 1–19). Cham: Springer. Retrieved from https://www.researchgate.net/publication/318853356_Sharing_Life_Stories_Design_and_Evaluation_of_a_Digital_Storytelling_Workshop_for_Older_Adults.

Jaroszewska, A. (2013a). Gdzie, jak i dlaczego polscy seniorzy uczą się języków obcych?. *Neofilolog*, *4*, 89–94.

Jaroszewska, A. (2013b). *Nauczanie języków obcych seniorów w Polsce. Analiza potrzeb i możliwości w aspekcie międzykulturowym*. Kraków: Oficyna wydawnicza "Impuls."

Jarvis, P. (2014). From adult education to lifelong learning and beyond. *Comparative Education*, *50*(1), 45–57.

Klimkova, B. (2018). Learning a Foreign Language: A Review on Recent Findings About Its Effect on the Enhancement of Cognitive Functions Among Healthy Older Individuals. *Frontiers in Human Neuroscience*, *12*(305), 1–7.

Kuchta, J. (2013). Seniorzy online czy offline? O wykluczeniu cyfrowym starszego pokolenia. *Studia Kulturoznawcze*, *2*(4), 165–178.

Marcinkiewicz-Wilk, A. (2016). Older people in the information society. *Journal of Education Culture and Society*, *7*(1), 18–31.

National Institute of Adult Continuing Education. (May 2015). A *Better Future for Us All: A Policy Paper on Older People and Learning National Institute of Adult Continuing Education*. Retrieved from http://stephenmcnair.uk/wp-content/uploads/2015/07/A_Better_Future_For_Us_All.pdf.

National Institute of Aging. (2007). *Why Population Ageing Matters. A Global Perspective*. Retrieved from https://www.nia.nih.gov/sites/default/files/2017-06/WPAM.pdf.

O'Keeffe, L. (2017). Performing the Soundscape With Third Age Adults: The Derry Soundscape Project. *Wi: Journal of Mobile Media*, *11*(1). Retrieved from http://wi.mobilities.ca/performing-the-soundscape-with-third-age-adults-the-derry-soundscape-project/.

OECD. (2019). *Elderly population (indicator)*. Retrieved from https://data.oecd.org/pop/elderly-population.htm.

OECD. (2017). *Pensions at a Glance 2017: OECD and G20 Indicators*. Paris: OECD Publishing. Retrieved from https://www.oecd-ilibrary.org/docserver/pension_glance-2017-en.pdf?expires=1561288014&id=id&accname=guest&checksum=BD5151CE48369FCEDAC35409F151C2B2.

Quinn, K. (2018). Cognitive Effects of Social Media Use: A Case of Older Adults. *Social Media + Society*, *4*(3), 1–9.

Repetto, M. & Trentin, G. (2008). Social networking and the third age. In M. Kendall & B. Samways (Eds), *Proceedings of the WCC 2008, Learning to live in the Knowledge Society, Milan 8–10 September.* (pp. 279–286). New York: Springer.

Siemieniecki, B. (2007). Komunikacja a społeczeństwo. In B. Siemieniecki (Ed.), *Pedagogika Medialna. Podręcznik akademicki. Tom 1.* (pp. 15–50). Warszawa: PWN.

Tarkowski, A., Mierzecka, A., Jasiewicz, J., Filiciak, M., Kisilowska, M., Klimczuk, A. & Bojanowska, E. (2015). *Taksonomia funkcjonalnych kompetencji cyfrowych oraz metodologia pomiaru poziomu funkcjonalnych kompetencji cyfrowych osób z pokolenia 50+.* Warszawa: Centrum Cyfrowe Projekt Polska.

United Nations. (2017a). *Ageing, Older Persons and the 2030 Agenda for Sustainable Development.* Retrieved from https://www.un.org/development/desa/ageing/wp-content/uploads/sites/24/2017/07/UNDP_AARP_HelpAge_International_AgeingOlderpersons-and-2030-Agenda-2.pdf.

United Nations. (2017b). *World Population Ageing 2017 – Highlights.* Retrieved from https://www.un.org/en/development/desa/population/publications/pdf/ageing/WPA2017_Highlights.pdf.

Ware, C., Damnee, S., Djabelkhir, L, Cristancho, V., Wu, Y-H., Benovici, J., Pino, M. & Rigaud, A-S. (2017). Maintaining Cognitive Functioning in Healthy Seniors with a Technology-Based Foreign Language Program: A Pilot Feasibility Study. *Front. Aging Neurosci*, *9*(42), 1–10.

Wrońska, M. (2017). E-meryt, czyli blogujący senior – raport z badań. *Zeszyty Naukowe Wyższej Szkoły Humanitas. Pedagogika*, *15*, 137–144.

Zych, A. (2017). *Encyklopedia starości, starzenia się i niepełnosprawności. A-G.* Katowice: Thesaurus Silesiae Katowice.

Zych, A. (2007). *Leksykon gerontologii.* Kraków: Oficyna Wydawnicza “Impuls.”

Lionel Nicolas
Eurac Research, Italy
Julia Ostanina-Olszewska
Pedagogical University, Kraków, Poland
Špela Arhar Holdt
University of Ljubljana, Slovenia
Claudia Borg
University of Malta, Malta
Jaka Čibej
University of Ljubljana, Slovenia
Verena Lyding
Eurac Research, Italy
Anabela Barreiro
INESC-ID, Portugal

Introducing an implicit crowdsourcing opportunity to teachers

Abstract: This paper aims at attracting attention towards crowdsourcing opportunities for the language teaching community. It presents and discusses a specific crowdsourcing paradigm designed to mass-produce exercise content for different languages by involving their language learners online. The discussion of the implicit crowdsourcing paradigm is framed by a broader look at the current situation regarding crowdsourcing and language learning. Therefore, we first introduce the concept of crowdsourcing, report on the teacher perspective and discuss common objections and practical challenges with regard to the compatibility of the language learning community with crowdsourcing in terms of expertise, motivation and feasibility. The implicit crowdsourcing paradigm we introduce proposes an approach for automatically generating language learning resources and, at the same time, crowdsourcing language-related datasets. It is designed to exploit a synergy between the language learning community and R&I partners working in language-related areas. The proposed approach is one of multiple experimental initiatives, which are being studied and explored within the enetCollect COST Action (European Network for Combining Language Learning with Crowdsourcing Techniques). We conclude the paper with a discussion on our efforts to raise awareness among the varied stakeholders so as to foster the creation of tools implementing the crowdsourcing paradigm.

Keywords: Implicit Crowdsourcing, Language Learning, Automatic Generation of Exercises, Teacher Survey, enetCollect

1. Introduction

Over the past decades, demands on L1 and L2 teaching in national and secondary education systems have undergone remarkable changes. Market globalization and increased migration flows due to geopolitical reasons have led to a diversification of learner profiles and needs. Accordingly, the effectiveness of the language learning material offered within many countries is at risk of gradually falling behind because of the heterogeneity of the target groups and new opportunities to enhance the production of language learning material should be explored. One such opportunity is crowdsourcing, a decentralized and community-driven/participatory approach that has allowed achieving impressive ground-breaking results in numerous domains. For example, Wikipedia[1] completely redefined the well-established domain of encyclopaedias and the reCAPTCHA[2] approach combined the identification of humans versus bots on websites with the transcription of hard-to-read text snippets, allowing to digitize vast amounts of text by obtaining an unparalleled and continuous workforce from the crowd.

The enetCollect[3] Action, a large European Research and Innovation (R&I) network funded as a COST Action,[4] pursues the objective to respond to the abovementioned language learning challenge by taking the first steps in combining the fields of language learning and crowdsourcing in order to foster the language skills of all diversified groups of language learners, regardless of their social, educational, and linguistic backgrounds. As a network project with

1 https://en.wikipedia.org/wiki/Main_Page
2 https://en.wikipedia.org/wiki/ReCAPTCHA
3 https://enetcollect.eurac.edu/
4 https://www.cost.eu/

several hundreds of members,[5] in enetCollect the R&I objectives are approached by its members through funded networking activities like meetings, trainings and short research stays concerned with the topic of language learning and crowdsourcing. It involves stakeholders from the language learning community and from language-related areas that can provide mutually-beneficial support in discussing demands and devising solutions to crowdsource learning materials and language-related datasets through language learning activities. The enetCollect community is grouped into five specialized working groups focusing on different types of crowdsourcing, language learning and legal, ethical and business aspects.

In order to incentivize concrete crowdsourcing applications for language learning, we present and discuss a crowdsourcing paradigm that allows mass-producing exercise content for different languages by involving language learners online. The presented paradigm relies on the expectation that several language learning exercises can automatically be generated from existing language-related datasets, such as lexica, and that learners' answers to these exercises can be used to improve the underlying datasets.

This paper is organized as follows. We discuss the state of affairs by reviewing the state of the art (Section 2), by briefly sketching the field of crowdsourcing (Section 3), and by presenting the results of a survey on crowdsourcing for language teachers (Section 4). We then discuss the compatibility of this community with crowdsourcing in terms of expertise, motivation and feasibility (Section 5), present the crowdsourcing paradigm (Section 6), and outline which concrete measures are taken to foster the creation of tools implementing it (Section 7), before summing up with a conclusion (Section 8).

2. Review of literature

The overall body of literature related to the combination of language learning and crowdsourcing techniques is rather scarce. In fact, enetCollect has been proposed to start filling this gap by launching a new R&I field around this topic and by bringing together related efforts from the language learning communities (e.g. CALL – Computer-Assisted Language Learning), from other language-related communities (e.g. NLP – Natural Language Processing) and from the crowdsourcing communities (e.g. HC – Human-based Computation).

---

5 In November 2019, around 260 persons were registered on the general mailing list and around 180 persons created a profile on the intranet.

However, when trying to situate our work within existing research fields some connecting points can be found. For example, by considering why crowdsourcing has only been seldom used within the language learning community, we can relate our work to studies about the language learning community itself with respect to the adoption of recent IT technologies on a wider scale (cf. e.g. of Voogt & Knezek 2008 and Eickelmann 2011), as discussed in Section 4 and 5 in more detail.

Also, the crowdsourcing paradigm presented in Section 6 shows similarities with the approach of the language learning platform Duolingo (Von Ahn 2013), which made use of automatically generated translations to generate exercises. A comparison of the two approaches is made in Section 6.5 after presenting the paradigm itself.

Because of its interdisciplinary and "cross border" nature, the work presented in this paper can also be partially situated within the existing field of CALL and HC or Implicit Crowdsourcing (IC) approaches. These fields have explored many approaches, which to various extents are relevant to our work. However comparing precisely our efforts to them would go beyond the scope of this paper. We nonetheless refer the interested reader to relevant efforts such as the ones of Kukulska-Hulme and Shield (2008), Kukulska-Hulme (2010) and Godwin-Jones (2011) for CALL, and, in the following section, we briefly sketch crowdsourcing and its multiple forms, including HC and IC.

3. Crowdsourcing in a Nutshell

Because of its relation to a crowd, crowdsourcing is sometimes confused with crowdfunding, an approach to fund initiatives of varied types (projects, start-up companies, music albums, etc.) by collecting small amounts of money from a crowd.

As distinct from crowdfunding, crowdsourcing relies on a crowd contributing not with their money, but with their time and knowledge. One could see crowdsourcing as the practical implementation of the proverb "Unity is strength." Ever since the term *crowdsourcing* was introduced by Jeff Howe in Wired,[6] it became the most buzz-generating of media buzz-words (Brabham 2013).

Although crowdsourcing is considered a creation of the Internet era (Bynum 2019), information-gathering projects with a considerable number of

6 https://www.wired.com/2006/06/crowds/

participants have existed for decades and served, for instance, for creating the Oxford English Dictionary (Brabham 2013). However, modern technological developments facilitating the access to the Internet and mobile applications allowed crowdsourcing to prosper in the past fifteen years, which led to numerous overlapping trends resulting in various crowdsourcing scenarios.[7] As far as enetCollect and language learning are concerned, the most relevant trends are "Wisdom-of-the-crowd" (WoC), "HC," "IC" and "Game-With-A-Purpose" (GWAP).

The WoC approach usually refers to a large scale, open-ended collaborative resource creation which is of common interest to a crowd of contributors. Wikipedia is a remarkable example in the context of encyclopaedias. The HC approach aims at crowdsourcing tasks that computers cannot solve properly. HC approaches usually gather data via so-called "micro tasks" distributed via platforms such as Amazon Mechanical Turk[8] and Crowdflower.[9] ReCAPTCHA is an example of the HC approach that asks users to input two words displayed as an image, preventing automatic bots to enter restricted parts of websites. This process assisted the digitization of parts of books on which optical character recognition (OCR) software failed. By not explicitly stating to the users the "secondary" use of the information they inputted, reCAPTCHA can be considered as an IC approach. In IC, a service is provided to a crowd, which creates the data of interest (e.g. Duolingo) by using the service. In GWAP, a particular type of IC approach, games are designed for collecting data from users playing the game (Chamberlain et al. 2013). The concept of *crowdsourcing* is also linked to *Citizen Science*[10] whereby a crowd of amateur scientists publicly participate with the aim of advancing scientific research and public understanding of science.

4. The survey: Teachers and Crowdsourcing

In order to investigate the possibilities of introducing crowdsourcing to language learning classrooms, we conducted a survey among language teachers of different languages and at different levels of education. As crowdsourcing techniques in the digital era are primarily conducted online and research has shown that teachers' use of ICT is guided by their attitude, competence, and access to technology

7 https://en.wikipedia.org/wiki/Crowdsourcing#Examples
8 https://www.mturk.com/
9 https://www.figure-eight.com/
10 https://en.wikipedia.org/wiki/Citizen_science

(Voogt & Knezek 2008), the survey included questions about: teachers' familiarity with the concept of crowdsourcing and their current experience with it, their attitude towards including it in their teaching, and the availability of required technology. These topics have previously not been addressed by the research community and present a valuable insight for the development of solutions tailored to the actual needs of teaching practitioners. The structure and sample of the survey are described in detail in Arhar Holdt et al. (2020). Here, we summarize the most relevant findings to establish background for the forthcoming discussion.

The survey was disseminated between June 2018 and February 2019 in over 30 European countries. From 1,698 language teachers who answered the first question of the survey, 1,129 completed it. The participants were aged 20 to 65, mostly working at institutions of tertiary education, followed by second/foreign language teachers. The survey comprised 17 closed-ended questions pertaining to (a) teachers organizing crowdsourcing activities for their students; and (b) teachers themselves participating as a crowd. An open-ended question asking for (c) additional comments, opinions and experience was also included. On the first page of the survey, a short definition of the term "crowdsourcing" was provided, together with some examples in order to establish a common understanding of the term.[11]

The results of the survey revealed that 23 % of the respondents organized an activity in which their students participated in crowdsourcing (see Figure 1). The respondents indicated a number of needs to address in order to facilitate such activities such as, among others, (a) concrete ideas about which specific activities would be suitable for their subject, and (b) tutorials about crowdsourcing-based teaching techniques. Frequently reported were the need for a pre-prepared lesson plan; a clear indication of motivational aspect or value for the students; and improved technical equipment. While crowdsourcing activities with students seem to be hindered by the lack of equipment and knowhow on how to approach the issue, teachers themselves seemed more experienced (Figure 2): 40 % reported participation in crowdsourcing activities

11 "This survey is about crowdsourcing – the practice of getting ideas or help on a project from a large number of people, usually through the internet. People participate voluntarily and the project is typically beneficial to the community. Some teaching-related examples of crowdsourcing include: preparing Wikipedia entries; adding subtitles with translations to educational videos (e.g. Khan Academy, TED); selecting, editing and sharing language examples for exercises or tests; sharing teaching materials on open digital platforms so other teachers can use them, etc."

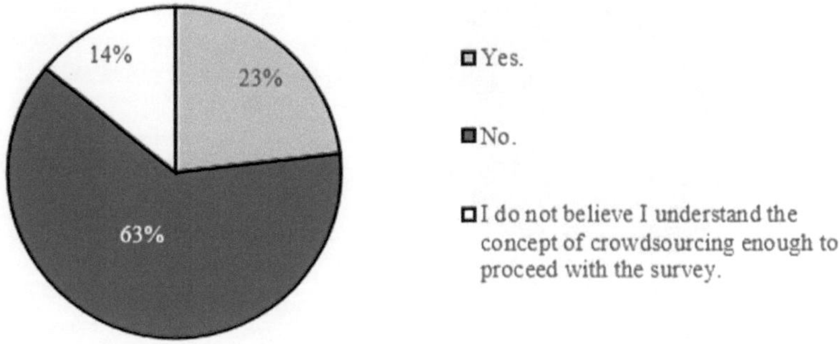

Figure 1. Have you ever organized an activity where your students participated in crowdsourcing? (Valid N = 1698).

such as sharing teaching materials on digital platforms or, to a lesser extent, through workshops, projects, conferences, blogs, university repositories and other online or offline means.

Pertaining to access to technology, 936 respondents reported on available equipment in their affiliated institution(s) as follows: availability of computer rooms (62 %), students' smartphones (56 %), and a classroom computer (52 %). Tablets, either student- or school-owned, were rarely available. Less relevant for crowdsourcing, still often mentioned were smartboards, whiteboards, overhead projectors, CD players, or a laptop owned by the teacher, while some respondents indicated that students had no access to technical equipment whatsoever.

Teachers showed a very positive attitude towards motivation for further participation, with only 4 % replying they would not participate[12] (see Figure 2). The most frequent motivational factors were (a) acquiring new skills and knowledge in the process, and (b) saving time in the long term on class preparation. Other motivational factors were the feeling to have contributed to a greater cause; professional accreditation; and finalized products as the result, e.g. a textbook or a dictionary. Accordingly, the most preferred crowdsourcing tasks were: (a) collaboration with other teachers in the creation of interactive digital learning materials and (b) selecting, editing, and sharing language examples for exercises or tests.

12 It should be noted, of course, that the teachers who participated in the survey naturally constituted a more positively inclined sample to begin with.

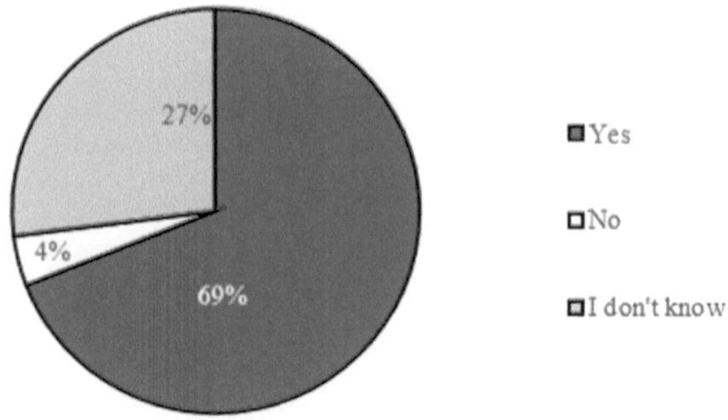

Figure 2. Generally speaking, would you be willing to participate in crowdsourcing teaching materials for the language(s) you teach (by preparing and providing useful content)? (Valid N = 924).

Open-ended comments summarized several important reservations, namely their current lack of training in crowdsourcing, lack of time and funds to be attributed to the new activities, as well as scepticism about the quality of content created via crowdsourcing. To conclude, the attitude of the teachers towards crowdsourcing is generally positive, while their desire for more information on matters such as crowdsourcing, tutorials, or ideas for implementation reveals that their competence needs to be improved. Furthermore, the limited access to technology should be taken into consideration when developing new solutions.

5. Teachers and Students as Crowdsourcers

When discussing crowdsourcing in a language learning context from a theoretical perspective, several doubts arise. The first is whether teachers and students constitute a valid crowdsourcing workforce in terms of competence and reliability for creating language-related materials. The second is the question of their motivation to contribute. The third is whether such implementation is feasible in terms of resources and equipment.

When it comes to competence, a crowd composed of teachers can hardly be questioned, as they are experts in the languages they teach. Learners, on the other hand, might seem as an unreliable source for crowdsourcing quality information on languages they have not mastered yet and in which they are likely to make mistakes. While this is a valid concern, it should be noted that many crowdsourcing approaches design tasks that can be solved even by non-experts without complex or specialized knowledge (Fort, et al., 2012). This is usually done by deconstructing a complex undertaking (e.g. part-of-speech annotation) into manageable micro tasks (e.g. Is "cat" a noun?) before handing them over to the crowd, meaning that tasks are always adapted to the level of competence of the target crowd (e.g. learners). Multiple responses to the same question by different persons are then cross-matched to achieve the final solution. Many crowdsourcing projects have already researched and implemented quality control methods to deal with issues of reliability, e.g. a gold standard dataset, inter-annotator agreement, intra-annotator consistency, and redundancy (cf. Poesio et al. 2017), which are also applicable in the language learning context. In addition, certain types of responses, particularly true-false judgments, can be successfully aggregated to obtain reliable results (see Section 6.3).

In terms of motivation, students are less problematic, especially if a crowdsourcing task can be linked to their primary motivation to learn a language. That is, if crowdsourcing tasks are designed with the students' educational goals in mind, they can simply substitute the tasks used in a traditional teaching environment. The motivation of teachers, however, is not inherent, but depends on their willingness to include crowdsourcing tasks in their lessons. While the results of our survey indicate that a majority of teachers is willing to contribute (see Section 4), they also indicated a need for a prepared lesson plan, as well as for basic training in crowdsourcing techniques. Motivation should thus not be an impeding factor preventing teachers from being involved in a crowdsourcing project. In fact, teachers as a group are comparable to other crowds participating in WoC projects; for example, many respondents in the survey stated that sharing teaching materials is something they already actively participate in, but on a much smaller and more restricted scale (e.g. with their colleagues). If teachers were provided with a crowdsourcing platform to collaborate on teaching materials with a large number of other teachers, a Wikipedia-type scenario is entirely possible.

While competence, reliability, and motivation do not seem to hinder the implementation of crowdsourcing in language learning, the main problem seems to be feasibility in current circumstances. Indeed, as the expansion of crowdsourcing is related to digital technologies, it has mainly been used in more technologically inclined fields (e.g. artificial intelligence, bioengineering, and NLP) and has so far bypassed fields such as language learning. In other words, the lack of crowdsourcing in a language learning context is likely to stem from the lack of crowdsourcing tools made available to them. In order to constructively address part of this issue, we introduce a generic IC approach with great potential for creating a number of such tools.

6. Combining Language Learning and Implicit Crowdsourcing

In this section, we introduce the "implicit crowdsourcing paradigm" as a generic approach particularly suitable for exploiting a synergy between the language learning domain and other language-related fields relying on language-related datasets (e.g. NLP). Despite the fact that the paradigm and the survey were developed independently from one another, one complements the other as the paradigm partially addresses the conclusions derived from the survey as it allows tackling the lack of crowdsourcing tools.

The power of implicit crowdsourcing approaches is that they reuse existing workflows of the targeted crowd in order to perform crowdsourcing while providing a relevant service. Indeed, as indicated by the term "implicit," the crowdsourcing is "hidden" within a workflow, which, on the surface level (user perspective) is offering an ordinary service. Reusing an existing workflow guarantees the usefulness and adoption of the service provided to the targeted crowd. Also, the familiarity of the crowd with a service implies that no particular training is needed for using this service, and thus for the underlying crowdsourcing. For example, reCAPTCHA (von Ann et al. 2008) adapted the existing workflow of the Captchas to digitize books while providing a service of human identification on webpages. In the context of language learning, a workflow we identified as most promising is the one where learners implicitly contribute by performing language learning exercises that are automatically generated for them.

We explain hereafter how crowdsourcing can be done by combining existing language-related datasets and well-known learning exercises. We then address the practical concerns of the approach, especially from the language learning perspective, and motivate the win-win synergy it exploits between the various stakeholders. Finally, for the sake of widening the scope, we also briefly sketch other workflows that could also be adapted to perform crowdsourcing in the context of language learning.

6.1. A theoretical paradigm for performing implicit crowdsourcing

So as to understand this paradigm, we first consider a concrete and implementable example: an exercise based on the concept of "Word Search," which is often used in learning tools such as the "Tell me more" suites,[13] where learners identify words in a grid of letters (see Figure 3).

13 https://www.tellmemorecampus.com/

Figure 3. An example of a Word Search game. https://en.wikipedia.org/wiki/Word_search.

The content for such exercise can be automatically generated from a lexically-oriented dataset such as an NLP lexicon. When generating the exercise, it would be possible to automatically add an extra word not described in the NLP lexicon (e.g. a neologism candidate extracted from a news feed). By doing so, the learners' answers can be used to gather insights on these newly added words. Indeed, if learners are asked to look for common nouns, any time a learner selects the extra word, the learner implicitly votes for it being a noun. Also, when a word registered in an NLP lexicon as a common noun is rarely selected by the learners, one can interpret it as learners voting for it to not be a common noun.[14] The ratio of the learners' answers on specific words can serve as basis for decisions on adding the words, or information about them, to the NLP lexicon, or removing them.[15]

The same type of analysis can be applied to other types of exercises that can be generated from existing language-related datasets. For example, an exercise on verb conjugations can be generated from morphological rules and can also allow double-checking the validity of these rules. An exercise asking a student to transform a sentence (e.g. to the active/passive form) can be generated

14 Given that the learners are familiar with the word, of course.

15 From a language learning perspective, the data could also be used to identify gaps in the learners' knowledge.

from a Treebank and can allow deducing what the learner believes to be the function of the words of the sentence (e.g. the subject, the object). This in turn can allow evaluating the validity of the entries of the Treebank. An exercise asking students to provide words by analogy (e.g. "yellow is to banana what green is to...") can be generated from a WordNet and, at the same time, can allow discovering new relations between words or evaluating the existing ones.

The overall reasoning can be generalized to the following theoretical paradigm:

IF one can generate an exercise from a language-related dataset,
THEN one can use the learners' answers to improve the dataset.

6.2. Practical concerns of the theoretical paradigm

So as to anticipate the scope and practical feasibility of this paradigm, five aspects should be considered.

- For how many types of exercises could the content be generated from existing language-related datasets?
- How can learners actually learn while being crowdsourced?
- What feedback should the system provide for questions for which the correct answer is not yet known?
- How can the answers of learners be a reliable source of information?
- How can the content be adapted to the needs of the learners?

Regarding the types of exercise content that could be generated from existing language-related datasets, we have carried out a small study of exercise types and language resources out there.[16] Given that numerous aspects of a language (ranging from morphological to syntactic and semantic aspects) are encoded in various types of datasets (morphological rules, lexica, treebanks, etc.), and the fact that learners have to master these same aspects of a language, we could identify existing datasets for many well-known exercise types and, as such, identify the possibility to implement many automatic mechanisms to generate their content.

Regarding the question how learners can actually learn while being crowdsourced, the answer is that they can only learn on the questions on which they are not crowdsourced on. Indeed, in all cases where the tool is asking questions that it does not know the answers for, the learners are the ones

---

16 http://videolectures.net/3rdAnnualActionMeeting2019_nicolas_crowdsourcing/

"teaching" the tool while it is supposed to be the other way around. An implicit crowdsourcing tool thus needs to strike a balance between learning from the learners (crowdsourcing) and teaching them in order to not impede their learning progression. This can be achieved by generating most questions from the reliable part of the dataset (i.e. the gold standard part) while generating only a few questions from unreliable parts or external resources (e.g. news corpora).

Regarding the feedback to provide for questions for which the correct answer is not yet known (e.g. when trying to figure out the grammatical category of a neologism), there is no single solution, as it depends on the setting of each specific exercise. One option can be to inform the learner that no reliable answer is available to the system while indicating the top-ranked answer candidate with a reliability score. Another approach can be to simultaneously ask the same question to several learners and crossmatch their answers in real time. A third solution can be to inform the user that he will receive feedback once a reliable answer has been identified. Also, informing users about their hidden crowdsourcing contribution and rewarding them, e.g. by providing a free language learning service, may foster their understanding for an occasionally limited or delayed feedback on exercises.

Regarding the question how the answers of learners can be a reliable source of information, the answer is that exercises need to be designed in a way that allows drawing conclusions regarding the correct answer, by combining multiple responses for the same question (by different learners in the crowd). For example, if a question has many possible answers (e.g. what do learners consider to be the lexical, syntactic and semantic properties of the verb *to consider*?), cross-matching the answers would prove harder. However, if the question can allow deducing, directly or indirectly, a "yes" or "no" judgement (e.g. Does the learner believe that "food" is a common noun?), then the reliability of the answers will range from 50 % (random answers) to 100 % (perfect understanding). This implies that each single answer, even the weakest ones with 51 % reliability of the student, will contribute to reaching statistical certainty. In other words, for questions where a yes/no judgment can be deduced, provided that a sufficient number of answers to the same question can be cross-matched, figuring out the right answer is statistically achievable.

Regarding the question about how to adapt the content to match the needs of learners, we can take inspiration from previous works that focus solely on automatically generating exercise content. In the presented paradigm, we just extend the original use case with a hidden mechanism to improve the underlying dataset. As such, all existing state-of-the-art strategies can be integrated with this approach.

6.3. A win-win partnership

The added value of the implicit crowdsourcing paradigm can be measured on the benefits it brings to its stakeholder groups, namely the language learning community and partners from language-related R&I fields (e.g. NLP researchers). From an abstract perspective these benefits are the same for both stakeholder groups: the paradigm helps to automatize tasks that are usually performed in a manual fashion, namely the creation of exercise content and the curation of language-related datasets.

For the language learning stakeholders, participating in a crowdsourcing collaboration built around the implicit crowdsourcing paradigm, allows "delegating" the creation of exercise content to an automatic mechanism devised to generate the exercises from language-related datasets. On a practical level this "delegation" means that the work of language teachers will shift from *handcrafting exercise content* to *defining what the exercise content should be like*, while R&I stakeholders take over the task of automatically producing content for the specified type of exercise from existing language-related datasets. Given the fact that the language-related datasets out there can easily be populated with millions of entries, the extent of exercise content that can be generated from them should exceed the amount of content that could be manually produced in a reasonable time frame.

For the R&I stakeholders interested in curating language-related datasets, the benefit of implementing the implicit crowdsourcing paradigm is the opportunity to "delegate" the curation of these datasets to the language learners instead of employing cost-intensive expert manpower. Given that worldwide the number of such R&I stakeholders is much smaller than the number of language learners,[17] we expect that such win-win partnerships could allow R&I stakeholders to obtain an unprecedented and continuous amount of data in expert quality on a scale comparable to what famous initiatives such as reCAPTCHA have accomplished for different crowdsourcing purposes.

Last but not least, we also expect that R&I stakeholders are likely to contribute to extending online language learning offers, not only by generating

---

17 According to our observations at conferences of language-related domains, numbers are in the range of several hundreds to several thousands, language learners can easily exceed hundreds of millions (see Europeans and their Languages, Special Eurobarometer 386 Report, http://ec.europa.eu/public_opinion/archives/ebs/ebs_386_en.pdf).

exercise content but also by improving other aspects of the language learning service in order to improve the service offered and thus the crowd of learners reached.

6.4. On-going implementations of the implicit crowdsourcing paradigm

As an innovative concept developed in the context of a COST Action, the paradigm is at present well defined as a theoretical concept, while the development of an explicit and consensual methodology for implementing it is still in experimental stage. In fact, a number of publications on the subject discuss and demonstrate directly or indirectly its viability, such as one on a generic architecture for implicit crowdsourcing with a vocabulary trainer application implementing it (Rodosthenous et al. 2020) and one presenting various resource generation scenarios by different NLP stakeholders (Nicolas et al. 2020).

Indeed, in Nicolas et al. (2020), the authors explain two things which prove that a viable context exists to implement the paradigm. Indeed, on the one hand, they report on a preliminary study performed on five English workbooks covering the six CEFR levels. In that study, they discovered that around 90 % of the types of exercises could theoretically be automatically generated from existing types of NLP datasets (even though the implementation of the generation mechanisms will certainly present for each some specific challenges), and that around half of the automatically generated exercises could theoretically be used to crowdsource useful information from the learners. In other words, many of the existing types of exercises have the potential to be used to implement the implicit crowdsourcing paradigm. However, on the other hand, the authors briefly sketch the numerous crowdsourcing scenarios explored by different NLP stakeholders. By doing so, the authors demonstrate that, on the NLP-side of things, there is at present a very favourable interest for devising paths of practical implementation of the implicit crowdsourcing paradigm.

Out of the aforementioned crowdsourcing scenarios explored, the implementation of a vocabulary trainer based on a generic crowdsourcing architecture has by now reached a certain maturity and was employed in different experiments with learners as documented by several publications (Rodosthenous et al. 2019, Lyding et al. 2019, and Rodosthenous et al. 2020). This scenario relies on the creation of a vocabulary trainer whose questions are generated from the common sense ontology ConceptNet and in which the answers of learners are used to improve ConceptNet. In this scenario, two types of questions are generated: open-ended questions where the learners are asked to provide a word that is semantically related to a word displayed (e.g. to name one thing related to "house"), or closed questions where learners are asked to evaluate if two words are related to one another (e.g. to answer if "house" and "home" are related). Such a scenario is possible since the data in ConceptNet and the knowledge that the learners aim at learning are actually of very similar nature: they both conceptualize the semantical relations between words. From one publication to the other, the authors gradually demonstrate the practical viability of the implicit crowdsourcing paradigm while they uncover and address several challenges related to the innovative and unexplored nature of their endeavour. For example, in their latest publication (Rodosthenous et al. 2020), the authors noted that an unforeseen bias in the automatic generation of their questions and in their grading system led learners to guess that "yes" is the more probable answer than "no" in most cases. Consequently, in case of doubts on the right answer, many learners chose to answer "yes" instead of choosing to not answer the question. Despite this crucial flaw in the system design, the latest results obtained are encouraging in two ways. First, despite the prototypical nature of the trainer and the flaws it still has at present, a collaborative effort by NLP and language learning researchers allowed creating a prototype that already has an educational value and that was in most cases well received by the group of learners it was tested with. Second, the results indicate that the answers of the learners can indeed be used to create expert knowledge and correct ConceptNet. Both achievements provide a concrete use case demonstrating the practical viability of the implicit crowdsourcing paradigm.

6.5 Other crowdsourcing-compatible existing workflows

In the previous subsections, we focused our attention on one promising implicit crowdsourcing workflow because of the strong synergy it exploits and the feasibility of its implementation. Nonetheless, we would like to stress that other workflows targeting a crowd of teachers and/or students can be devised.

For instance, the common workflow of teachers correcting student essays could be reused to crowdsource learner corpora (corpora of annotated learner essays), which allows for empirical studies of most typical learners' language problems. The workflow of teachers correcting exercises that can be automatically generated but not automatically corrected (e.g. reading comprehension exercises) could also be used to crowdsource valuable data (e.g. the main subject of an article).

6.6 The implicit crowdsourcing paradigm with respect to the state of the art

To our knowledge, the related state of the art is limited to the approach of the language learning platform Duolingo (von Ahn 2013), which made use of automatically generated translations to generate exercises. Such exercises in turn allowed Duolingo to crowdsource useful answers for evaluating the quality of the translations. In our case, we aim at automatically generating exercise content and crowdsourcing useful language-related data, as explained in the sections above. The key differences with Duolingo's approach are twofold.

First, whereas Duolingo devised exercises for the sake of crowdsourcing a predefined type of data (i.e. translations), we focus on reusing existing and well-established exercise types in order to ensure their relevance for learning.

Second, Duolingo was collecting data for business purposes, whereas our aim is to collect data to enhance R&I in language learning and language-related fields, such as NLP, Learner Corpora or Corpus Linguistics. In other words, the data we collect primarily benefits directly the crowd of language teachers and learners we rely on and indirectly the larger public, by enhancing language-related R&I fields, which are mostly created by publicly funded institutions such as universities.

6.7. Context to make the combination between language learning and implicit crowdsourcing happen

So as to exploit the implicit crowdsourcing paradigm and mass-produce both exercise content and language-related data, two conditions have to be met: the creation of language learning tools implementing such paradigm and their actual use by learners.

As discussed in Section 6.3, from a theoretical point of view, there are good reasons for all related stakeholders to invest efforts in such an initiative. From a practical point of view, however, a sufficient awareness of the approach and its potential as well as a concrete and practical context to work on it are needed to make it happen. In particular, it is crucial to create an interdisciplinary network of all stakeholders in order to shape the language learning tools in a way that objectives and needs of all related R&I stakeholders are considered. This is particularly true for carefully addressing language learning aspects when automatically generating exercise content.

We believe that the COST Action enetCollect is providing the grounds to address both parts. Indeed, COST Actions are currently one of the largest European R&I mechanisms for bringing together researchers and R&I

stakeholders (e.g. through funded networking meetings), for developing shared objectives and tackling them (e.g. through small funded scientific exchange visits), and for creating visibility within the community and beyond (e.g. by disseminating intermediate outputs to a wide audience).

Thus, as a large and busy COST Action,[18] enetCollect provides the context and funding to involve a critical mass of R&I stakeholders. EnetCollect members have already started numerous efforts (some addressing the implicit crowdsourcing approach, such as Rodosthenous et al. 2020) resulting in a number of new publications and funded projects.[19]

Regarding the involvement of language learners and teachers, enetCollect is implementing an indirect approach. Indeed, during meetings and through dissemination activities, including presentations at conferences, enetCollect reaches out to stakeholders (e.g. teacher trainers) that can act as a bridge to language learners and teachers in order to create awareness of the ongoing works, test prototypes or disseminate the newly created solutions.[20]

Such "bridging" stakeholders are large language learning platforms (e.g. Busuu, Duolingo or Babbel), R&I partners or stakeholders attending language-learning-related conferences and reading related publications (i.e. researchers and teachers with an interest in new developments) such as this one. EnetCollect also reaches out to them by means of conference presentations (e.g. at EUROCALL 2018 and 2019, and at PL-CALL 2019) and by inviting key stakeholders to its meetings (e.g. Busuu[21]).

Another type of "bridging" stakeholders are R&I-friendly teachers which are not R&I stakeholders. Up to now, in enetCollect this was the most difficult group to involve. An initiative in their direction was the teacher survey (Section 4), which also served to raise awareness and create visibility of our

---

18 By November 2019, enetCollect has built a community of around 260 R&I stakeholders from 39 different countries, has organized 10 meetings and 2 training schools with a total number of more than 450 participants and funded more than 35 research stays. Also, it has received high grades for its midway evaluation.

19 More precise information on these aspects can be found directly on the website of enetCollect or in the report of the midway evaluation mentioned previously.

20 Prototypes are often the result of small research collaborations among members, which tackle their specific interest (e.g. crowdsourcing Multi Word Expressions – MWE) that are often tested via experiments involving their target groups (e.g. learners).

21 http://videolectures.net/3rdAnnualActionMeeting2019_campbell_howes_acquisit/

activities. In addition to follow-up surveys,[22] we also foresee to establish a dedicated mailing list to maintain teachers informed of progress in the combination of language learning and crowdsourcing, and to create targeted dissemination material (such as videos, tutorials or flyers) to convey the developed knowledge, first practical achievements and outputs as well as opportunities for active participation.

7. Conclusion

In this paper, we discussed crowdsourcing opportunities for the language teaching community and more specifically, a crowdsourcing paradigm designed to mass-produce exercise content by involving language learners online.

We started with a broader perspective by discussing the outcomes of a survey on crowdsourcing distributed to numerous teachers and by reflecting on the compatibility in terms of expertise, motivation and feasibility of a crowd of learners and teachers with crowdsourcing approaches. We observed that many crowdsourcing approaches would be suitable for such crowds and that the absence of such crowdsourcing efforts is probably due to the fact that language learning had not received enough attention from technology-oriented stakeholders capable of implementing such modern technologies.

We then introduced the crowdsourcing paradigm and explained why it has the potential to mass-produce content for a variety of exercises. We also addressed the issues that one would meet when implementing it in practice and provided explanations on how to overcome them.

Finally, we discussed the measures taken to raise awareness among the relevant stakeholder groups in order to foster the implementation of such a paradigm in practice.

We believe that the efforts and knowledge described in this paper constitute a short-term and concrete milestone towards a long-term objective of great potential for the language learning community and other language-related fields. We thus conclude this paper by inviting the interested readers in joining us in our efforts[23] to address the next milestones.

---

22 A learner-oriented survey is in preparation.

23 https://enetcollect.eurac.edu/joining-enetcollect/

8. Acknowledgements

This article is based upon work from COST Action enetCollect (CA16105), supported by COST (European Cooperation in Science and Technology).

References

von Ahn, L. (2013). Duolingo: learn a language for free while helping to translate the web. *Proceedings of the 2013 International Conference on Intelligent User Interfaces, Santa Monica, USA*. ACM, New-York, 1–2.

von Ahn, L., Maurer, B., McMillen, C., Abraham, D. & Blum, M. (2008). reCAPTCHA: Human-Based Character Recognition via Web Security Measures. *Science*, *321*, 1465–1468.

Arhar Holdt, Š., Zviel-Girshin, R., Gajek, E., Durán-Muñoz, I., Bago, P., Fort, K., Hatipoğlu, Ç., Kasperavičienė, R., Koeva, S., Lazić Konjik, I., Miloshevska, L., Ordulj, A., Rodosthenous, C., Volodina, E., Weber, T. & Zanasi, L. (2020). Language Teachers and Crowdsourcing: Insights from a Cross-European Survey. *Rasprave*. Institut za Hrvatski Jezik i Jezikoslovlje, Zagreb. (In print).

Brabham, D. C. (2013). *Crowdsourcing*. Cambridge MA: MIT Press.

Bynum, L. J. (2019). Crowdsourcing. *Salem Press Encyclopaedia*.

Chamberlain, J., Fort, K., Kruschwitz, U., Lafourcade, M., & Poesio, M. (2013). Using games to create language resources: Successes and limitations of the approach. In I. Gurevych & K. Jungi (Eds.), *Theory and Applications of Natural Language Processing* (pp. 3–44). Berlin/Heilderberg: Springer.

Eickelmann, B. (2011). Supportive and hindering factors to a sustainable implementation of ICT in schools. *Journal for Educational Research Online*, *3*(1), 75–103.

Fort, K., Nazarenko, A. & Rosset, S. (2012). Modeling the Complexity of Manual Annotation Tasks: a Grid of Analysis. *Proceedings of the International Conference on Computational Linguistics (COLING), Mumbai, India*. Association for Computational Linguistics, Santa Fe, 895–910.

Godwin-Jones, R. (2011). Mobile apps for language learning. *Language Learning and Technology*, *15*(2), 2–11.

Kukulska-Hulme, A. (2010). Mobile learning as a catalyst for change. *Open Learning: The Journal of Open and Distance Learning*, *25*(3), 181–185.

Kukulska-Hulme, A. & Shield, L. (2008). An overview of mobile assisted language learning: From content delivery to supported collaboration and interaction. *ReCALL*, *20*(3), 271–289.

Lyding, V., Rodosthenous, C., Sangati, F., ul Hassan, U., Nicolas, L., König, A., Horbacauskiene, J. and Katinskaia, A. (2019). v-trel: Vocabulary Trainer for Tracing Word Relations – a Crowdsourcing Approach. *Proceedings of the International Conference Recent Advances in Natural Language Processing (RANLP), Varna, Bulgaria.* INCOMA Ltd. Shoumen, Hissar, 675–684.

Nicolas, L., Lyding V., Borg, C., Forascu, C., Fort, K., Zdravkova, K., Kosem, I., Cibej, J., Arhar Holdt, S., Millour, A., König, A., Rodosthenous, C., Sangati, F., Ul Hassan, U., Katinskaia, A., Barreiro, A., Aparaschivei, L. and HaCohen-Kerner, Y. (2020). Creating Expert Knowledge by Relying on Language Learners: a Generic Approach for Mass-Producing Language Resources by Combining Implicit Crowdsourcing and Language Learning. *Proceedings of the 12th Edition of the Language Resources and Evaluation Conference (LREC),* Marseille, France.

Poesio, M., Chamberlain, J. & Kruschwitz, U. (2017). Crowdsourcing. In N. Ide & J. Pustejovsky (Eds.), *Handbook of Linguistic Annotation* (pp. 277–295). Dodrecht: Springer.

Rodosthenous, C., Lyding, V., Sangati, F., König, A.,ul Hassan, U., Nicolas, L., Horbacauskiene, J., Katinskaia, A. & Aparaschivei, L. (2020). Using crowdsourced exercises for vocabulary training to expand Conceptnet. *Proceedings of the 12th Edition of the Language Resources and Evaluation Conference (LREC)* (pp. 307–316). Marseille, France.

Rodosthenous, C., Lyding, V., König, A., Horbacauskiene, J., Katinskaia, A., Ul Hassan, U., Isaak, N., Sangati, F. & Nicolas, L. (2019). Designing a prototype architecture for crowdsourcing language resources. *Proceedings of the Poster Session of the 2nd Conference on Language, Data and Knowledge (LDK)*(pp. 17–23). Leipzig, Germany.

Voogt, J. & Knezek, G., (2008). IT in primary and secondary education: Emerging issues. In J. Voogt & G. Knezek (Eds.), *International Handbook of Information Technology in Primary and Secondary Education* (pp. xxix--xxlii). New York: Springer.

Online sources

https://en.wikipedia.org/wiki/Main_Page

https://en.wikipedia.org/wiki/ReCAPTCHA

https://enetcollect.eurac.edu/

https://www.cost.eu/

https://www.wired.com/2006/06/crowds/

https://en.wikipedia.org/wiki/Crowdsourcing#Examples

https://www.mturk.com/

https://www.figure-eight.com/

https://en.wikipedia.org/wiki/Citizen_science

https://www.tellmemorecampus.com/

https://en.wikipedia.org/wiki/Word_search

http://videolectures.net/3rdAnnualActionMeeting2019_nicolas_crowdsourcing/

http://ec.europa.eu/public_opinion/archives/ebs/ebs_386_en.pdf).

http://videolectures.net/3rdAnnualActionMeeting2019_campbell_howes_acquisit/

https://enetcollect.eurac.edu/joining-enetcollect/

Robert Oliwa

The Bronisław Markiewicz State School of Technology and Economics, Jarosław, Poland

Reshaping translation competence for the competitive online economy: action research

Abstract: The aim of this chapter is to determine if and how undergraduate English studies students are prepared to offer translation services in the changing online economy. Moreover, the study attempts to establish what modifications to the existing study programmes should be introduced in order to cater for both students' and customers' needs. The group included twenty three 3rd students of English in Business and Multimedia specialization with some introductory translation experience. The implementation and delivery of the instructional content occurred during regular translation and computer assisted translation classes. The study used action research design and lasted from January until May. Results indicate that undergraduate English studies students lack certain skills and competences as far as technological skills and service provision are concerned. This may be improved by introducing new courses or modifying the existing ones. These encompass specialist language courses, grammar and style, start-up business courses, quality control and work placement programmes. The conclusions drawn from the action research suggest that augmenting the present programme of studies with the new content may develop the students' translation competence and, therefore, help them to stand out in job market.

Keywords: translation, services, computer, assisted, undergraduate

1. Introduction

The contextualization of the process of translator[1] training in order to suit the competitive digital economy and align it with the possibilities the internet is

1 In this chapter, the term *translator* will be used to cover both the area of translating and interpreting because it is the author's belief that, as far as undergraduate skills and translation competence are concerned, the two areas overlap. Indisputably, differences in skills between the two are greater than their similarities. While linguistic and cultural competence is still vital, the most important quality of a good translator is the ability to convert meanings and concepts well from a source language into the target language in writing. Interpreting, in turn, is the art of listening to

bringing about has attracted a lot of attention over the last decades. The very translation instruction is founded and developed on the assumption that it should reflect the real world and the tasks it provides. Therefore, it may help students to adjust to challenges the job market creates. They are engaged in a simulated business-like offline or online tasks where they practice providing translation services and where a translated text is a commodity which undergoes various stages students are accountable for (Olvera-Lobo et al. 2005). Different tasks are delegated to students in various models of instruction and they are evaluated on the process of task completion and the very final service they accomplish. However, translator training reaches far beyond the confines of a single discipline which developed from a solid language core. Besides, it relies on a number of interconnected and structured skills as so to serve the initial aim of training a competent translator. The area of translator training, or preferably education as it involves longitudinal process of competence building and contribution of a number of professionals, has long been recognized. The reason why the author objects to the idea of commercial training courses, which promise to prepare a competent translator over a period of two to four weeks, is that it is not feasible to equip a language student with an appropriate set of skills to translate or interpret texts. Translation students must rely on model translators who will assist them systematically in the search for knowledge, not information, with their experience, competence, skills but also the portfolio of translated texts (Broś 2014). Translation training in order to provide expected outcomes must derive from a multitude of areas, namely language and culture studies, business studies, psychology, technology or work placement programmes to name only a few (Kiraly 2013; Albir & Taylor 2015). New contributors which have an impact on the way and methods of translator instruction come onto the stage ceaselessly, however two of them seem to be the most significant players, i.e. computer technology and the job market itself. The former because of the amazing array of tools and applications it offers; the latter owing to its global and specialized nature.

The development of translator training has undergone considerable adjustments to the very process and stages of translation and the final product it tries to develop and sell. The following part of the chapter will look at how the theory and practice of the translator training have changed and consider the proposed models and programmes of instruction.

---

a speaker in a source language, grasping the meaning and next paraphrasing the understanding of the meaning using the tools of the target language.

2. Translation theory and translator training

Unsurprisingly, recent years have observed the growth of translator training programmes at different levels throughout the world. Researchers have paid a lot of attention to the very phenomenon and consequently put a considerable amount of effort into researching the fields of translation and translator training (Gwóźdź 2016). The quotation from Shreve (in Kiraly 1995: X) explains the intertwining nature of the theoretical and practical translation:

> A pedagogy of translation has to derive from an understanding of translation reality. If we define translation reality, at least for the sake of the present argument, as what translators do and what translators produce as both practice and product then translation theory is the description and explanation of practice and product. A translation pedagogy without a theoretical basis will be a blind pedagogy. It will fail to set reasonable objectives, will be unable to create and apply methods appropriate to the learning task, will be unable to measure and evaluate re-suits, and will ultimately fail to create the effective translators our society increasingly demands.

The practice and theory of translation contradict one another and at the same time justify their existence and functions. Particularly significant is the connection between translation theory and translation practice which both have an enormous impact on translation didactics nowadays (Piotrowska 2007). Translation theory, being part of the area of linguistics, attempts to prescribe the methods and tools which can be employed in the process of finding equivalents of meanings of one language into another (Klemensiewicz 1955). Despite translation being a rather ancient discipline, starting with bilingual vocabulary lists in Sumerian and Eblaite, then Greek and Latin works translated into national languages, the pedagogy of translation per se is a recent field of study, although questions such as *Will translation theory be of use to translators?* (Levy 1965) or *is the theory of translation of any use to translation practitioners*? are still valid. According to Gile (1995), a small amount of translation theory can only help if it is relevant, approachable, structured and recycled. Moreover, the theory of translation helps to describe and evaluate the constructs translators make. There seem to be two major approaches. The first one, from the historical perspective, claims that solid theoretical foundations are indispensable and have a tremendous impact on the contextualization as well as the function of translation. The other one, more contemporary, supported by the changing job market, the EU policy[2] as well as different

2 Translation services are available in the majority of EU institutions, e.g. in the European Commission, the Council, the European Parliament, the Court of Justice,

programmes[3] emphasizes the interdisciplinary character of translation and teaching key competences to translators. Polish translation studies, although relatively slow to introduce modifications until the 1960s, are now on a par with other countries when it comes to quipping translation students with the theoretical foundations and key competences (Szubert 2008; de Bończa-Bukowski & Heydel 2013). The development of the key competences seems to be the driving force behind the modern-day translator training; however, it reflects the initiatives developed by foreign languages methodology. These included the Grammar Translation Method, Direct Method, or Audiolingual Method but also more contemporarily psychological and learning theories such as cognitivism, constructivism and connectivism. Obsolete methods and teaching techniques (e.g. the Grammar Translation) or analysis of translation errors are being replaced with projects (task-targeted assignments), simulations, specialist translation and the use of problem solving techniques. The 21st century has witnessed numerous initiatives which have put translator training into a new context. One of the most pioneering ideas is the European Master's in Translation framework (EMT)[4], which outlines the elementary competences that translators have to acquire to work in today's labour market. The foremost aim of EMT is improving the quality of translator training to suit

---

the Economic and Social Committee, the Court of Auditors. The chief EU agency responsible for the multilingual communication needs of the EU agencies and other EU bodies is the Translation Centre for the Bodies of the European Union.

3 An interesting example of a translation programme is *Juventus Translatores*, a competition to reward the best young translators in the European Union. The 2019 session is an online translation contest for secondary EU schools. Each selected school enter 2–5 participants. Schools register students' names and their chosen language pairs (the language from and into which they intend to translate) on the Contest Platform by 15 November 2019. Students log in simultaneously to the contest platform with their individual username/password. Once participants are logged in, they can see the source text in their chosen language on their computer screen. They can then type their translation of the text. Once they have finished or the contest time is up, participants must save and submit their translation on the contest platform. More information is available at European Commission/Juvenes Translatores website. Other translation programmes and contests include *St. Jerome Translation Contest*, *Warwick Prize in Undergraduate Translation* or *Tłumacze na start*! at Tischner European University.

4 European Master's in Translation is a quality label for MA university programmes in translation (https://ec.europa.eu/info/resources-partners/european-masters-translation-emt/european-masters-translation-emt-explained_en).

the requirements of the changing market (Biernacka-Liczar 2011; Biel 2017). Besides, it integrates young translation professionals throughout European countries. The EMT competence framework (see Figure 1) is comprised of five subcomponents. The first one, *language and culture*, focuses on the knowledge of grammatical and lexical structures as well as the ability to understand and use them. Moreover, it corresponds to the knowledge of the rules for interaction in a specific cultural context and how to produce the suitable register. Another subcomponent, *translation*, relies on strategic, methodological and thematic competences which are employed and overlap during the process of translation. Next, the *technology* subcomponent, describes an efficient and skilful use of computer/internet tools which are applied for text search, translation assistance and more recently collaborative translation. The *Personal and interpersonal* subcomponent deals with personality traits and behaviours which help improve time and stress management, adaptability, cooperation and employability. Finally, *service provision* encompasses the knowledge of the business of translation including how to market services, negotiate with a client, manage budget and handle required documentation. The framework recognizes that translation services cover many areas of competence and skills necessary to translate meanings from one language to another and many different tasks carried out by those who provide those services (Thunnissen 2015).

The framework is founded on the principle that translation is a process planned to address the needs of different parties such as a translator, client or organization involved in it (Klimkowski 2015). Training competent translators in close cooperation with potential employers is consistent with the EU priorities and more and more universities, also outside the EU, use it as a model for designing their translation programmes.

The question which may arise after the analysis of the available instruction models concerns the pathways to achieving translation competence and its subcomponents. These may include process-oriented translation assignments which reflect requirements the market imposes rather than taking the product-oriented approach. Similarly, the problem-oriented approach may be adopted to enable the students of translation to better prepare for the forthcoming workplace challenges (Vienne 1994). Another perspective is the learner-centred approach, which takes into consideration individual learners' differences as well as preferences; where the student is in charge of learning and self-reflection while the tutor facilitates the learning of translation. In addition, there is the situated learning approach, which perceives translation competence through translation problem-solving activities in repeated real live (unfamiliar) language situations (Kiraly 2013). Last but not least, the available offline and online computer/

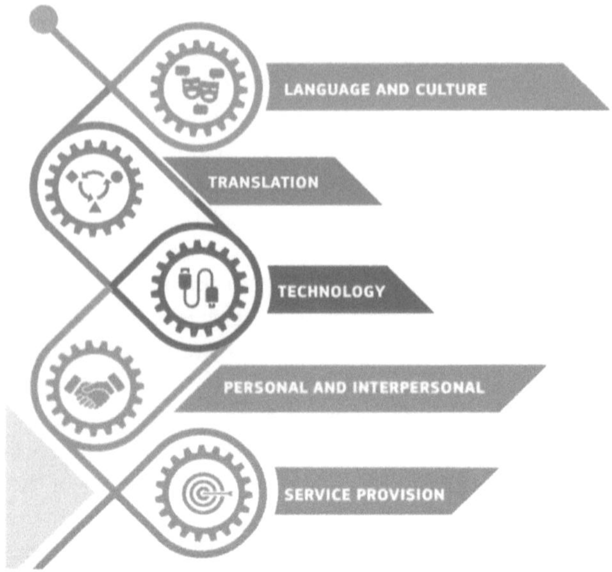

Figure 1. The European Master's in Translation framework.
Source: EMT Competence Framework – 2017.

internet tools allow the facilitation of translation training during shared tasks and projects as well as expose trainee translators to available resources.

Until now, translator training, particularly for undergraduate students, does not seem to have been comprehensively investigated. Nor has a design for translator instruction been unambiguously supplied. Consequently, there is a need to study and research if and how students are prepared to provide translation services in the changing online economy. Moreover, attempts should be made to establish what changes to the existing study programmes are required in order to address both students' and customers' needs. Providing a comprehensive translation road map which presents objectives, deliverables, resources and timeline may have an influence on students' performance, including the students who study translation for employment reasons. Above and beyond, a study programme giving details of the training on a timeline, responsibilities, update stages, and detailed view of the training progress can also contribute to the results students achieve. The stakeholders of instruction design process, i.e. teachers, students and ordering parties should have an equal share and be of equal importance during the design process. Consequently, a negotiable shared space could be set up so as to satisfy different needs and expectations as to translator training (Klimkowski 2015).

The following study attempts to contextualize and link the EMT model with the available undergraduate translation studies and find out how to equip students with an appropriate set of competences.

3. The Study

3.1. Aim and the questions

The chapter aims to present an account of a translation project, its outcomes and follow-up undertakings included into regular undergraduate English studies at State Higher School of Technology and Economics in Jarosław (Państwowa Wyższa Szkoła Techniczno-Ekonomiczna w Jarosławiu).

The study addressed the following research problems:

1. Why did an online project not facilitate undergraduate students' translation competence to offer translation services?
2. How may the increased students' exposition and access to translation resources and the application of online tools equip translation students with the requisite competences for the work market?

The data were collected with the aim of answering the two research questions and determining if augmenting regular translation programme for a period of five months (January – May 2019) may help to enhance and modify the programme of translation studies of English in Business and Multimedia specialization with introductory translation experience. Likewise, an analysis and assessment of the project and its follow-up were carried out in view of the achieved results, instruction method and future recommendation and modifications.

3.2. Participants

The group who took part in the study consisted of twenty three 3rd year undergraduate students of English in Business and Multimedia specialization, 13 women and 10 men. The group had had some introductory translation experience gained during the 2nd year of studies. The studies programme they were following intended to help the students acquire knowledge and skills to find employment in different state and private institutions and companies including translation services. Having completed the studies they are expected to acquire primary competence to interpret and translate oral and written texts from Polish into English and vice versa.

3.3. Research context

Students of the researched specialization take general courses (physical education, information technology, sociology, ethics, intellectual property), practical English skills (reading, listening, speaking, writing, practical phonetics, practical grammar), core subjects (descriptive grammar-morphology, descriptive grammar-syntax, introduction to linguistics, project workshops, intercultural communication, interculturality in international corporations, introduction to literature, history of English literature with elements of British and American life and institutions, glottodidactics, European systems of language competence), specialist translation courses (communication in business, written and oral translation, media translation, business translation, technical translation, information technologies) and the internship which students complete after year 2. Finally they take the general German course. The degree takes three years to complete. Despite the fact that e-learning/b-learning component can be implemented, it is not available for any of the courses.

The translation project, which started in January 2019 prior to the beginning of the new academic term (see Figure 2), embraced business and technical translation courses continued from the previous term and a new course, which was added to the programme of studies, i.e. computer assisted translation in translation. The project was an initiative to enable the students to offer competent translation services in the changing online economy. The initiative involved a simulation of an online translation agency run by the students with the teachers' supervision. It was discussed with the students who expressed their readiness to take part in it as they considered it a hands-on experience compared to the regular classroom-based courses. They divided themselves into teams, each of which dealt with different areas of a translation agency activity, namely website design, marketing, customer service and social media.

After the introductory phase the students joined different specialist translation groups (see Figure 3) and agreed to report to the teachers on their progress on a weekly basis.

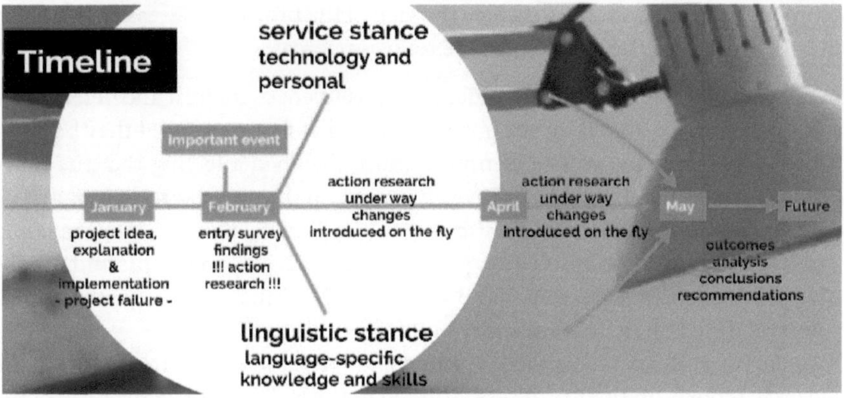

Figure 2. Project timeline.

Figure 3. Translation project website.

3.4. Observation

One month after the commencement of the translation project, based on the observation and results of the teams' work, interviews, students' comments, and their attendance, it became apparent that after the initial eagerness it would fall through and realizing its aims (improving the students' translation competence) would not be possible. The lack of the project progress enabled the authors to look for the problem in the following areas:

- engagement: it referred to the students' inquisitiveness, interest and determination when they worked on the goals. Although at first motivated they became disengaged over the course of time because they had a feeling that the individual involvement would not have an impact on the overall group progress.
- skills: this area refers to linguistic and cultural knowledge, translation competence, computer technologies, personal and interpersonal skills and finally labour market requirements. The students lacked the skills required or felt overwhelmed by their complexity and relationships.
- supervision: the students were granted a lot of autonomy in their work with weekly reports on their progress. This led to the lack of control over the main aims of the project and eventually students' poor task and time management.
- the unknown: providing online translation services, as indicated by the students, was a novelty for them. Despite the fact that they are digital natives, the students had no experience of e-work which implied the use of communications technology to work remotely from home. They did not know what software or applications to use to e-work.
- aims: although the global aims for the translation project were specified, there were no objectives defined for each group to complete by a certain deadline. Furthermore, no group heads were appointed who would manage task management and contact other groups for updates.

3.5. The reason for the research

The research came about as a response to the failure of the project and consequently the lack of the development of the students' competence, skill and readiness to provide translation services. It also aimed at studying the project follow-up and augmentation to provide translation services in a professional context (starting from client-customer relationships through to project supervision and quality management) within the translator training. As a result, the research also addressed the question of how translation studies may be streamlined and improved. Another examined was the language-specific knowledge and skills which will be discussed in a separate article.

3.6. Techniques and analysis of collected data

The action research design was applied the aim of finding the reasons for the translation project non-success. It also enabled observation, examination, reflection and streamlining the translation training, and the augmentation of the programme of studies with the new content so as to develop the students' translation competence. Moreover, it allowed the authors to investigate and share their own practice, classroom activity where the very journey was as exciting as the destination itself (Cravo 2007). The research included such tools as observation, field notes, survey, interview (screening, formative and reflective) and check lists. The language resources were delivered in class and in an online content management system (CMS). The final part consisted of the translator's portfolio where students could display a showcase of their work and learn how to promote their services. The task started with the discussion about the methods and places where translators could promote and advertise their translation services. The anticipated outcome was an online translator's portfolio which each student was required to embark on. The portfolio had a tabbed interface with sections such as *about me*, *work samples*, *services* and *contact me* to enable the students to publish record of their work.

3.6.1 Preliminary data analysis

The surveys carried out at the onset showed that 26 % of the students sometimes translated texts in return for remuneration and 61 % rarely had an opportunity to translate outside regular classes. The remaining 13 % never translated anything except in class. An interview denoted that in terms of the computer and information technologies the most developed skills included the use of search engines (Google Chrome, Mozilla Firefox, Internet Explorer), text editing, file management and the least developed skill displayed was the use of translation software. Moreover, it was discovered that the students did not create their own traditional or computerized databases of translated texts, attend conferences or workshops on translation; nor did they use any printed resources. The only place where they seek for translation tools was the internet (see Figure 4).

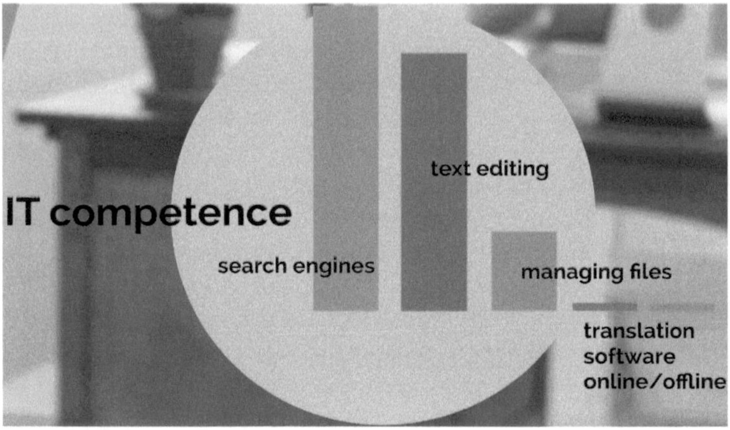

Figure 4. Students' areas of IT competence.

It was also revealed that the only translation-related website the students were familiar with was Google Translate, which was further confirmed in the area of online translators, dictionaries and computer-assisted tools. Finally, a multi selection survey carried out among the students revealed that 22 % did not intend to apply for employment as translators, 57 % planned to work in other areas and translate if an occasion arose, 22 % wanted to teach English[5] and only 4 % of the students aspired to take up employment in translation services. As the majority of the students had no regular translation practice outside classes, additional resources were published online, in the CMS.[6] They included business translation activities and tasks, sample materials, presentation of CAT tools key features and application instruction manuals.

5 The chosen major did not grant them officially required qualifications to teach English.

6 The CMS used for both business translation and CAT classes was Google Classroom which is a free service for schools, non-profits and anyone with a Google account. It helps learners and instructors to connect, inside and outside classes. Google Classroom is designed to help teachers create classes, distribute assignments, communicate and stay organized online. It also integrates other Google apps including Google Docs, Gmail, and Google Calendar.

3.6.2 Postliminary data analysis

The analysis of the available data shows that the increased students' exposition and access to both printed and online resources as well as the application of new translation tools improved the following areas.

The biggest increase was achieved as far as frequency of translation was concerned where over the period of five months 9 students (39 %) had a go at a regular translation employment. Similarly to the initial result, 3 students never attempted to translate outside regular classes (see Table 1).

Table 1. Frequency of students' translation outside regular classes.

	The number of students who undertook translation work		
	Before	After	
regularly	0 %	39 %	• freelancing • temporary employment contract • fixed term contract
sometimes	26 %	48 %	
rarely	61 %	0 %	
never	13 %	13 %	

No considerable differences were noted as far as the most developed IT skills were concerned; these included the use of search engines (Google Chrome, Mozilla Firefox, Internet Explorer), text editing and file management. However, all the students were observed to acquire, critically evaluate and apply translation software and available CAT tools.[7] The most popular was MateCat voted the top translation tool for both individual and shared work by 100 % of the students. Next, came DeepL (56 %), Context Reverso (38 %) Ozdic (38 %), Wordfast Anywhere (26 %). Unexpectedly, 12 students (52 %) still admitted to using Google Translate to start a translation process and to verify the outcomes with other tools. Moreover, the students were observed to share more frequently online resources, process and manage different file formats. Finally, they reported their introduction to the basics of cloud (MateCat) and machine translation (OmegaT) and their role in the translation process.

7 These included MateCat, OmegaT, Wordfast Anywhere, DeepL, SmartCat, Ozdic, Context Reverso.

The research also aimed at the assessment of the students' readiness to undertake employment and offer translation services in response to the arranged activities. Hence, the students were interviewed about the subjects and courses which helped them tackle the challenges of the work market. In a multi selection survey 100 % of the students agreed that the most useful translation course was computer assisted translation, 92 % said it was specialist technical translation and 71 % decided it was specialist business translation. A better understanding of the tools as well as more in-class practice, in consequence, might have an impact on the change observed as far their employment preferences were concerned at the beginning of the action research and later on at its completion (see Figure 5).

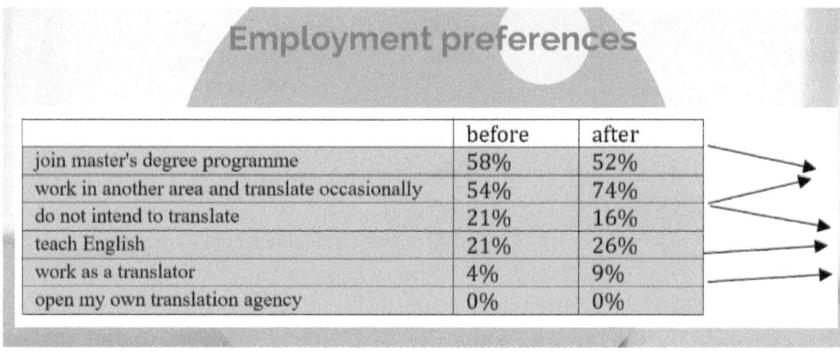
Employment preferences

	before	after
join master's degree programme	58%	52%
work in another area and translate occasionally	54%	74%
do not intend to translate	21%	16%
teach English	21%	26%
work as a translator	4%	9%
open my own translation agency	0%	0%

Figure 5. The change of the students' employment preferences.

The most important change concerned the students who intended to offer translation services. First, the number of the students who did not aim to translate at all decreased from 21 % to 16 %. 74 % of the students considered working as translators occasionally (20 % increase) and another 9 % planned to offer full time translation services (5 % increase). The number of students who meant to join master's degree programmes declined from 58 % to 52 %. Additionally, more students expressed their willingness to teach English despite not having formal qualifications to offer such courses. No students intended to open their own translation office both at the beginning and end of the research.

The final part of the action research required the students to create an online translator's portfolio (see Figure 6). When asked about their opinions about it, the students said, e.g.:

The portfolios helped me display a showcase of my work.
It helps me gain a competitive edge.
It increases my credibility by showcasing tangible evidence of the level of my translation.
It required no financial investment.[8]
It may provide a friendly platform for the interaction with customers.

Figure 6. A sample homepage of a student's portfolio.

In addition, as it turned after in-class task presentation and analysis, 91 % of the students accessed the CMS resources, completed the tasks, and later reported on them in class. Such an improvement may result from the improved language competence and computer skills, effective translation strategies, better understanding of the market demands and its awareness or finally enhanced project management.

The final task which revolved around a translator's portfolio indicates that considerable progress was achieved not only as far as technology competence was concerned but also in the area of service competence which further had an impact on the overall translation competence. This could result from the students' belief that translation is not indispensable to provide translation services which is very practical by its very nature and may largely depend on experience and work record. It might be a direct consequence of the lack of

8 The students used Portfoliobox, a free tool for creating online portfolio websites which its users like for its simplicity and intuitiveness.

start-up business courses and the students' ignorance of legal as well as fiscal requirements to launch such an office.

Finally, the students voiced the following major recommendations about the existing course and programme of studies:

The computer assisted translation course should be introduced at an earlier stage of the training process.[9]
Start-up business courses can be included as optional courses.[10]
The courses which are not related to translator training should be removed and hours of work placement programmes ought to replace them.

4. Conclusions

The research aimed at discovering, first of all, why an online project failed to facilitate undergraduate students' translation competence to offer translation services. Second, it examined how the access to translation resources and the application of online tools can prepare translation students for the work market. The reason for the project failure may stem from the students' lack or little development of the key competence areas which included *language and culture*, *translation*, *technology*, *personal* and *interpersonal* and *service provision* to translate meanings from one language to another and carry out different tasks. Moreover, the observed difficulties may be a result of the students' disengagement, task complexity, no control over the main aims of the project, no experience or their poor task and time management. The proposed action research can be considered valuable in showing how over a period of time translation skills and competences were modified on account of planned activities. The introduction of the computer assisted translation course may appear to have been the most pivotal factor which contributed, first, to the increase of the amount of translation practice the students did either regularly or sometimes outside systematic in-class training. Second, the students expanded the range of translation software whose application and features they were acquiring through various tasks. In addition, the students could develop such transferable skills as teamwork, critical thinking time and task management or thinking outside the box. As regards the provision of translation services, the students could identify the courses which would contribute to the improvement

9 At the time of the research the computer assisted translation course started in the last term of Year 3.
10 The main emphasis was put on running online business.

of their translation proficiency or which they considered impractical. Besides, they might gain confidence about their employment preferences, one of which was translator's work. Finally, the portfolio project could have an impact on the students' better understanding of how to promote their services and increase chances of gaining new customers.

Further to the above mentioned conclusions, the proposed action research was found to be valuable in finding a solution to a specific problem and planning an intervention to remedy it. It is the author's belief that the foremost assets of the research are related to the indications that undergraduate translator training requires further development and modification which might be beneficial for both students and their environment. A lot has been written and discussed about the theory and practice of teaching translation. This, however, has not resulted in creating a unified, binding concept of translation studies. Thus, we are facing a challenge which is intriguing and worth tackling. Translation competence is a complex system of simultaneous, interconnected, structured elements which complement one another and together may lead to proficiency. In order to offer reliable translation services students have to undergo systematic training which bridges the gap between theory and practice. As this research indicates, translation training also has to take under consideration such areas as computer literacy and service provision. The former encompasses all the knowledge and skills to implement computer assisted translation at different stages of the translation process. This may include machine, open source cloud-based, online or desktop translation tools. Universities offering translation studies should ensure students' access to commercial translation software to show the complete picture of the tools the translation market requires. Also, this area comprises computer skills to publish and market content online, business skills to define customer, budget, manage projects and quality and finally (inter)personal skills to teamwork, manage stress, time and deadlines, self-improve and update skills. To meet the requirements of the job market specialist computer courses for translators should be made compulsory in the programmes of studies. The latter area of service provision encompasses client-customer relationships, project supervision and quality management. The research showed that the programme of studies lacks business courses and they are not available at any level or in any form. Such a situation should be reviewed and areas such as working as a freelance translator, working with translation agencies, selling services, marketing in translation and targeting potential customers are required be included in the programme of studies.

The limitations of the presented research might relate to a small sample of participants, length of the study or the research model per se. Therefore, a further study is suggested which would include a larger sample of students or use quantitative and qualitative research methods. Alternatively, a structured model of translation competence implementation could be worked out, based on the existing knowledge, which would serve as the template for different parties to refer to.

References

Albir, A. & Taylor, P. (2015). The Acquisition of Translation Competence. Competences, Tasks, and Assessment in Translator Training. *Meta: Journal des traducteurs*, *60* (2), 256.

Biel, Ł. (2017). Quality in institutional EU translation: Parameters, policies and practices. In T. Svoboda, Ł. Biel & K. Łoboda (Eds.), *Quality aspects in institutional translation* (pp. 31–57). Berlin: Language Science Press.

Biernacka-Licznar, K. (2011). Kształcenie tłumaczy specjalistycznych w sieci EMT. Sprawa kellgrena – przykład. Nabywania kompetencji tłumaczeniowej. *Rocznik przekładoznawczy. Studia nad teorią, praktyką i dydaktyką przekładu*, *6*, 132–149.

Broś, K. (2014). Studenci w dobie Internetu i skomputeryzowanego rynku pracy: jak dostosować studia translacyjne do zmieniających się realiów. *Lingwistyka Stosowana, 11*, 11–28.

Cravo, A. (2007). Action Research in Translation Studies. *The Journal of Specialised Translation*, *7*, 92–107.

de Bończa Bukowski, P., Heydel, M. (Eds.) (2013). Polska myśl przekładoznawcza. Badacze, teorie, paradygmaty. In: *Polska myśl przekładoznawcza Antologia.* Kraków: Wydawnictwo Uniwersytetu Jagiellońskiego.

European Master's in Translation (2017). Available at https://ec.europa.eu/info/resources-partners/european-masters-translation-emt/european-masters-translation-emt-explained_en. [Access: 24 April 2019].

Gile, D. (1995). *Basic Concepts and Models for Interpreter and Translator Training.* Amsterdam/Philadelphia: John Benjamins.

Gwóźdź, G. (2016). Translatoryka. Umiejscowienie, rola, kierunki rozwoju, zadania. *Zagadnienia Naukoznawstwa*, *2* (208), 251–247.

Kiraly, D. (2013). Towards a view of translator competence as an emergent phenomenon: thinking outside the box(es) in translator education. In D. Kiraly, S. Hansen-Schirra & K. Maksymski (Eds.), *New Prospects and Perspectives for Educating Language Mediators* (pp. 197–224). Tübingen: Narr Verlag.

Kiraly, D. (1995) *Pathways to Translation: Pedagogy and Process.* Kent: Kent State University Press.

Klemensiewicz, Z. (1955). Przekład jako zagadnienie językoznawstwa. In M. Rusinek (Ed.), *O sztuce tłumaczenia* (pp. 97–97). Wrocław: Zakład Narodowy im. Ossolińskich.

Klimkowski, K. (2015). *Towards a Shared Curriculum in Translator and Interpreter Education*. Wrocław: Wydawnictwo Wyższej Szkoły Filologicznej we Wrocławiu.

Levý, J. (1965). Will Translation Theory be of Use to Translators? In W. Wolfgang (Ed.), *Übersetzen* (pp. 77–82). Frankfurt/M.: Athenäum.

Olvera-Lobo, M., D., Castro-Prieto, M., Rosa., Quero-Gervilla, E., Muñoz-Martín, R., Muñoz-Raya, E., Murillo-Melero, M., Robinson, B., Senso-Ruiz, J., A., Vargas-Quesada, B., Domínguez-López, C. (2005). Translator training and modern market demands. *Perspectives: Studies in Translatology, 13* (2), 132–142.

PACTE (2011). *Results of the validation of the PACTE Translation Competence Model: Translation Project and Dynamic Translation Index*. London: Continuum, 30–56.

PACTE (2005). *Investigating Translation Competence: Conceptual and Methodological Issues*. META 50(2): 609–619.

Piotrowska, M. (2007). *Proces decyzyjny tłumacza. Podstawy metodologii nauczania przekładu pisemnego*. Kraków: Wydawnictwo Naukowe Akademii Pedagogicznej.

Szubert, R. (2008). Uniwersytecka dydaktyka przekładu w Polsce i za granicą. *Rocznik przekładoznawczy, 3/4*, 315–329.

Thunnissen, L. (2015). *The Framework and other models: comparison to PACTE and EMT. The PACTE-model*. The PETRA-E meeting. Misano.

Vienne, J. (1994). Toward a pedagogy of "translation in situation". *Perspectives, 2*(1), 51– 59.

Anna Turula

Pedagogical University, Kraków, Poland

Civic literacy in the telecollaborative language classroom

Abstract: The chapter looks at how civic literacy, as defined in Morgan (2016) can be effectively integrated into a virtual exchange (VE) based on the analysis of eTwinning projects carried out in Polish schools. The questions asked in the process are: What socially important problems make it into virtual exchanges carried out at school? What are the levels of integrating language and content in such a VE? What – if any – are the tendencies in such task design? For the purpose of answering these questions, one hundred eTwinning tasks were studied and 51 were chosen for further analysis as regards their design, links (seamless or not) between language and content as well as the themes that their authors see as worth propagating. The chapter presents the results of such an analysis, conclusions and teaching implications for the integration of citizen issues in VEs.

Keywords: virtual exchange, telecollaboration, civic education

1. Introduction

New Vision for Education. Unlocking the Potential of Technology, a report published by the World Economic Forum in 2015, lists six foundation literacies for the 21st century: literacy and numeracy; scientific literacy; ICT literacy; financial literacy; cultural literacy; and civic literacy. These literacies can be treated as the guidelines for or seen as the purposes of the modern education. As a result, all schools which want their students to navigate the modern world successfully should include these literacies in their curricula. When it comes to the language classroom, this seems to be best done through Content and Language Integrated Learning (CLIL), which hinges on the assumption that the development of the literacies mentioned above is the content taught through language. Out of the six, the present chapter concentrates on civic literacy as defined in *Partnership for the 21st c. skills* (2009 cited in Morgan 2016: 2):

> The knowledge and skills to participate effectively in civic life through knowing how to stay informed, understanding governmental processes, and knowing how to

exercise the rights and obligations of citizenship at local, state, national, and global levels.

In terms of further inspirations, all the considerations presented here revolve around Byram's (2008) proposal that a way forward for schools is to turn education towards democratic citizenship.

The chapter starts by presenting a growing interest in civic literacy, even if labelled differently (raising civic awareness, democratic education, etc.). It also reviews publications-to-date on how and how successfully such content may be integrated with language education. Then it presents a study on how different aspects of civic literacy are developed in eTwinning projects. The investigation focuses on the topics of such exchanges and the specifics of task design. The chapter closes with conclusions on how well eTwinning projects integrate civic content with language learning and how this form of education can be further improved.

2. Review of literature

The six foundation literacies listed by the World Economic Forum in their 2015 report (cited above) can be found throughout other educational prognoses. The Economist Intelligence Unit in their *Worldwide Educating for the Future Index* (2018) write about the need for a number of skills: interdisciplinary; creative and analytical; entrepreneurial; leadership; digital and technical as well as global awareness and civic education. Very similarly, the 2018 OECD report, *The Future of Education and Skills. Education 2030*, argues for the need of education aimed at inclusive growth based on equitable access to health, civic engagement, social connections, education, security, life satisfaction, and environment.

Table 1. Education for the future. Focus on the civic literacy.

World Economic Forum (2015) LITERACIES	**OECD Education 2030 (2018) EDUCATIONAL FOCI**	**Worldwide Educating for the Future (2018) SKILLS**
• literacy and numeracy • scientific literacy • ICT literacy • financial literacy • cultural literacy • **civic literacy**	• health • **civic engagement** • social connections • education • security • life satisfaction • environment	• interdisciplinary skills • creative and analytical skills • entrepreneurial skills • leadership skills • digital and technical skills • **global awareness and civic education**

As Table 1 shows, the prognoses overlap in several areas, emphasizing the importance of: ICT/technical/digital literacies, financial/entrepreneurial skills, or cultural/social connections. However, what they all include is the focus on good citizenship in the education of and for the future. This seems to be more than a hint for the 21st-century school. The question important to pedagogy – particularly to language pedagogy, which is the focus of the present considerations – is if the contemporary classroom can raise to this challenge.

A proposal that it can and should was made a decade earlier by Byram (2008): the way forward is to turn language education towards what is called democratic citizenship. Translating this general claim into classroom specifics, many of which go hand in hand with the definition of civic literacy cited earlier, Byram (2010: 320) argues for educating learners for active citizenship through enhancing the linguistic purpose of language teaching "by attention to the linguistic competence needed in social action and intercultural citizenship." Explicating it further, he promotes integration of language and content, based on the assumption that:

> …the content in question should draw on citizenship education, enriching it with attention to intercultural communicative competence and giving substantial and meaningful content to language lessons while providing opportunities for methodological innovation and cross-curricular cooperation. The acquisition of intercultural citizenship competences would be the aims and objectives realising both educational and instrumental/functional purposes. (Byram 2010: 320)

Such a teaching philosophy, as pointed out by Finardi (2015), implies a participatory approach – inspired by the work of the Brazilian educator, Paulo Freire (1970) – aimed at developing civic (critical) education *through* language or, as put by Beacco et al. (2010), understood as language *in* and *for education.* A model fulfilling the pedagogical requirement functions in glottodidactics is known as CLIL (Content and Language Integrated Learning). Recently, in the context of the globalized, connected world, the participatory approach to language education may also require, as Finardi (2015) adds, the development of the digital literacy to the level enabling "the use of technologies such as the ones used in social networks, wikis, blogs, smart phones and their applications" (p. 329). Language teaching methodology has an answer to this as well: CALL (Computer Assisted Language Learning).

Research into how CLIL and CALL methodologies inform and support the civic turn in language education is scarce. Anyway, what has been published on the topic of foreign language *in* and *for* civic education, enhanced with new technologies, offers some interesting insights into the feasibility of such a digitally-enhanced language-and-content merger.

Porto and Byram (2015) describe a telecollaborative project demonstrating how the introduction of subject matter and principles from citizenship education into the foreign language classroom can combine objectives from – and give meaning to – both, extending citizenship education beyond the local and the national foci owing to the use of new technologies. The findings of the study carried out alongside the project show that both the teachers and the students engaged in such education are prepared to change the focus of their lessons as well as their attitudes, even though the effects may not be uniform: *some* learners did identify with their transnational community and *some* learners became involved in their own local communities as a result of the project.

Other studies show that the application of CLIL to civic education – even in the simplest format, in which the content is drawn from the civics syllabus – poses a certain challenge. In Sandberg's study (2015), which focuses, among others, on teaching civic education through a foreign language, the interviewed teachers admit that such education is fraught with linguistic unpredictability. However, the problem, as they claim, could be solved by defining the genres for in-class analysis in the process of syllabus construction as different kinds of media discourse (news, opinion texts, accounts of current issues) and by preparing the students in advance for in-class interaction or by pre-teaching vocabulary. Another solution, which Sandberg puts forward in a later publication is "involving students in the design of CLIL study programmes, possibly both at lesson and programme level" (Sandberg 2017: 40).

However, what seems to be the most interesting observation based on research-to-date is that relying on CLIL in turning language education towards the development of civic literacy – or democratic citizenship (Byram) – does not have to mean that the content integrated in the process needs to be borrowed from the civics syllabus. Coral-Mateu (2013) shows that social and civic competences can be learned in the PE-in-CLIL class. His study demonstrates that students in such a class assume responsibilities when participating in a team; consider the benefits and risks associated with sport; demonstrate respect for individual differences and performances; and accept both losing and winning with dignity and respect. Brady (2013), in turn, argues that a change in attitudes towards democratic citizenship can be achieved by how in-class interactions are shaped. He writes:

> Proponents of a democratizing education argue that people who are given freedom and choice will eventually become better democratic citizens simply because they have learned how to negotiate with others, to identify obstacles and paths of resistance, to know themselves and others. They are also open to change and listening to

> others as they all consider themselves to be vital to the development of a vibrant and healthy social threefolding. (Brady 2013: 76)

The threefolding, as Brady argues, are the economic, the rights-responsibilities, and the spiritual-cultural spheres, which benefit from social classroom life and study. This is because, in reference to a much earlier publication by Prodromou (1992), what and how the educator imparts shows his/her view of the world, with its power relations and sense of authority. This implicitly shapes and is reflected by the attitudes of the students. In other words, it is the democratic teachers who make democratic citizens, both in the class s/he teaches and beyond. And since, to quote Byram (2008), citizenship is also about reflecting upon oneself and the society, a classroom which prepares for it (Barnett 1997, 2000 cited in Brady 2013: 76–77) provides students with opportunities to: reflect on their thoughts and actions; reinterpret the curriculum as a set of possibilities and practical hopes and not as an imposition; and develop sceptical and questioning outlook on their individual and collective learning.

All in all, the review of literature offers some insights into how the language classroom informed by CLIL and CALL methodologies can implement Byram's (2008) postulate to turn education towards democratic citizenship by developing civic literacy in its both aspects defined in Morgan (2016): knowledge and participation. These insights enable the formulation of a set of general guidelines on the way in which civic literacy approach can be integrated into the language classroom. Such guidelines include: (i) introduce relevant genres and pre-teach formal language necessary to discuss civic issues in the target language; (ii) promote democratic relations in the classroom; (iii) combine civic education with raising intercultural awareness and educate in and outside the classroom walls, globalizing the process, preferably through telecollaboration. What is scarce and requires further investigation are specific solutions such as task design as well as systemic ways of integrating civic and language education. The present chapter hopes to initiate filling in this gap. It does so by looking at language education through eTwinning (telecollaborative) projects. The choice is motivated by an assumption that such a form of schooling by its very character – cross-curricular, promoting reflection as well as action, developing intercultural communicative competence, internationalizing education, enhanced by ITC – has great potential in the area studied.

3. Study: method, data presentation and discussion

The aim of the study is to explore ways in which civic literacy can be developed in the language classroom by integrating broadly understood *civic* content into it. Particular attention is paid to one systemic way in which such a merger is successfully implemented: projects carried out as part of the eTwinning programme where the language-content integration is enhanced with technology used for telecollaboration. Particular attention is paid to specific solutions, such as task design in accordance with CLIL methodology as well as – following the guidelines related to classroom democratic relations cited in Section 2 – issues such as intercultural communicative awareness, digital literacy and the participatory approach. All this has been translated into the following research questions:

- *What civic themes are focused on in eTwinning projects? How cross-curricular are the tasks?*
- *What format/s of task design and student-student interaction is/are used in the projects?*
- *What aspects of digital literacy are developed in eTwinning projects?*

3.1. The method

Answers to these questions were sought through an ethnographic analysis of 100 chronologically most recent eTwinning Poland exchanges, available at https://etwinning.pl/kategoria/ciekawe-projekty/ (accessed 15.05.2019). The focus was on emergent trends in areas delineated by the questions rather than on numbers, in view of further, more profound investigation, which is now in progress.

3.2. The data and their analysis

Out of the 100 exchange projects analysed, 51 covered themes that could be qualified as pertaining to or developing civic literacy. They included care about the quality of life, responsibility for the common context, local and global, as well as digital literacy.[1] These themes translate (in order of popularity) into the following topics focused on in the exchanges studied:

- economy (money, business, jobs) (10);
- healthy lifestyle and well-being (10);
- Europe and beyond (9);
- tradition, history and heritage (6);

1 Since all 100 projects involved telecollaboration, all could be qualified as developing digital citizenship. The selection of the 51 was made based on the assumption that just using ICT in education does not make one a self-aware digital citizen.

- online safety (6);
- environment (5);
- action in crisis/charity (4);
- dealing with cyberbullying (3);
- promoting readership (3);
- equality (3).[2]

Table 2. Emergent trends in eTwinning projects; in order of pedagogical craftsmanship.

PROJECT DESIGN	COLLABORATION MODE	DIGITAL LITERACY	SUBJECT INTEGRATION
a series of separate products **25**	national teams+presentation **11**	different tools **31**	just foreign language **2**
the main product (often preceded by minor products) **6**	national teams+exchange+ feedback **3**	different literacies (explicit) **10**	foreign language as a means of communication plus a range of subjects **27**
the main product b based on minor products **15**	international teams working on products **22**	different literacies (implicit) **10**	crosscurricular **22**
a series of different products required in the gamified reality **5**	international teams working on complex products/solutions **15**		

When it comes to emergent trends observed in the 51 exchanges, there are four areas in which they were noted: the design of the project in terms of task sequence and its coherence; the way in which groups were formed and the interaction patterns they followed; the aspects of digital literacy developed in the course of the project; and the degree of project cross-curricularity. They are presented in Table 2, in an order which reflects their complexity understood in terms of pedagogical sophistication and craftsmanship.

When it comes to task design, it has been assumed that the least complex will be the projects in which the theme was the only linking element to a series of otherwise unconnected, simple tasks. There were 25 exchanges following such a design model out of the 51 analysed. A step up, pedagogically, is a more elaborate project, often preceded by minor tasks serving as warm-up (6 projects of this type). Coherence of such design grows, if the minor task(s) are what the main project challenge/outcome can capitalize on. Such a model is also more demanding in terms of teaching skills, and, as such, is placed higher in the

2 The numbers do not add to 51 as some projects had multiple foci.

hierarchy of emergent trends (15 projects). Top of the category is an eTwinning model whose design requires the highest pedagogical craftsmanship: creating an alternative reality in which the challenge facing the students is gamified and all tasks are smoothly incorporated in such a reality (5 such projects).

The collaboration mode, another trend focused on in the exchanges analysed, can also be ordered based on complexity, here understood as the intricacy of management and the interaction patterns. At the bottom of the category, we can place projects carried out in national teams and summed up by a series of presentations, usually in a videoconference between/among the participating classrooms (11 projects fitting the description). A slightly more complex mode involves such a mode enriched by feedback on the final product offered by partner classes (3 such projects). Then we enter a different level of pedagogical craftsmanship, with tasks involving international teams, which are much more difficult to manage but offer richer interaction and stronger focus on intercultural communication. Such mixed teams may work on final products (22 projects of this kind) or complex outcomes, some of which may even amount to solutions to various multifaceted problems (15 projects involving such collaboration mode).

As regards digital literacy, its development may be limited to creating tech-comfort with the ICT tools needed in a particular exchange (31 such projects). Still, it may also go beyond mere usage of the new media, into issues of internet safety, copyright or digital responsibility; issues requiring a more sophisticated pedagogy. Such issues may be treated explicitly (10 tasks of this type) or through such task design – pedagogically even more demanding – which brings the issues up implicitly, as part or a by-product of the outcome the teams are working on (10 projects of such design).

Finally, there are varying levels of complexity as regards the cross-curricularity of the projects studies. The exchange may be uni-focal, by relying on the development of language skills only (2 such projects). It may also integrate content from other subjects (27 projects of this type) or be broadly cross-curricular, satisfying syllabi of most/all subjects on the school programme (22 projects). The growing complexity implies increasing difficulty of coordination of the teachers involved as well as the intricacy of task design – enhancing with the amount of content to be integrated in the project.

3.3. Discussion

Answering the first two questions, we can say that eTwinning exchanges focus on a number of civic topics and are cross-curricular in doing this. This makes them a perfect answer to Byram's (2010) postulate, as they meet it on many different planes. They integrate developing different aspects of civic literacy with language learning through the themes they focus on. Owing to their telecollaborative character, they also "enrich it with attention to intercultural communicative competence." Finally, they are predominantly crosscurricular and definitely meaningful as they show it is possible to use the language learned with a purpose that goes beyond the classroom in many different ways.

When it comes to the different telecollaboration modes, the two preferred ones seem to be national/international teams working on a task. The latter mode definitely reinforces the attention paid to intercultural communicative competence postulated by Byram (2008, 2010). It is pedagogically comforting that this mode proved to be the most popular in the exchanges studied. However, in the light of Brady's claim (2013) about the importance of classroom interaction in changing the attitudes towards democratic citizenship, it seems that the international cooperation on a complex task or aimed at developing a solution to a multifaceted problem (collaboration modes much less frequently chosen) could create a context for more effective civic learning by creating a larger number of opportunities for learning "how to negotiate with others, to identify obstacles and paths of resistance, to know themselves and others." In this sense, beneficial as the programme already is, its participant teachers may be encouraged to turn towards more complex and demanding collaboration modes.

Finally, when it comes to the different aspects of digital literacy developed in the eTwinning projects, it has to be noted that most tasks are limited in this area to creating tech-comfort of the use of the ICT tools needed for task completion. It is the minority of projects that take digital literacy beyond the purely technical level into realms that could qualify as education for digital citizenship. Such realms include awareness of digital dangers, including cyberbullying, respect for copyright or a sense of civic responsibility of one's online actions. This being possible to be implemented in both explicit and implicit ways opens the window of opportunity to teacher creativity and task-design craftsmanship. This, together with teacher awareness of the need to take digital literacy beyond the purely technical use of the new media, seems another recommendation to be made.

4. Conclusions

Summing up the present study, it can be said that eTwinning exchanges provide the most promising answer to the postulate of integrating civic literacy into the language classroom. The 51 projects analysed fulfil most of the requirements of a successful merger of this kind. However, there seems to be a need to raise the awareness of the teachers willing to undertake such telecollaborative pedagogy as to the benefits of task design complexity as well as the fact that digital literacy goes way beyond the purely technical ICT expertise.

References

Barnett, R. (2000). *Realizing the University in an Age of Supercomplexity.* Buckingham: SRHE and Open University Press.

Barnett, R. (1997). *Higher Education: A Critical Business.* Buckingham: SRHE and Open University Press.

Beacco, J.-C., Byram, M., Cavalli, M., Coste, D., Cuenat, M.E., Goullier, F., & Panthier, J. (2010). *Guide for the development and implementation of curricula for plurilingual and intercultural education.* Strasbourg: Council of Europe Publishing.

Brady, A. (2013). Integrating the Spiritual-Cultural, Rights-Responsibilities, and Economics of a Citizenship Development Higher Learning through a Differently Conceived and Practiced Sociology in (Second Language) English in the Japanese University. *Creative Education*, *4*(12B), 75–82.

Byram, M. (2010), Linguistic and Cultural Education for *Bildung* and Citizenship. *The Modern Language Journal*, *94*, 317–321.

Byram, M. (2008). *From Foreign Language Education to Education for Intercultural Citizenship.* Clevedon, UK: Multilingual Matters.

Coral-Mateu, J. C. (2013). Physical education and English integrated learning: How school teachers can develop PE-in-CLIL programmes. *Temps d'Educació, 45*, 41–64.

Finardi, R.K. (2015). Current Trends in ELT and Affordances of the Inverted CLIL Approach. *Studies in English Language Teaching*, *3/4*, 326–338.

Freire, P. (1970/2007). *Pedagogy of the Oppressed.* New York: Continuum.

Morgan, L. A.. (2016). Developing Civic Literacy and Efficacy: Insights Gleaned Through the Implementation of Project Citizen. i.e.: inquiry in education: Vol. 8: Iss. 1, Article 3. Retrieved from: http://digitalcommons.nl.edu/ie/vol8/iss1/3. [Access 15 May 2019]

New Vision for Education Unlocking the Potential of Technology Industry Agenda. Prepared in collaboration with The Boston Consulting Group 2015. http://www3.weforum.org/docs/WEFUSA_NewVisionforEducation_Report2015.pdf.; access 15 May 2019.

Partnership for 21st Century Skills. (2009). P21 framework definitions. Retrieved from http://www.p21.org/storage/documents/P21_Framework_Definitions.pdf.

Porto, M. and Byram, M. (2015) A curriculum for action in the community and intercultural citizenship in higher education, *Language, Culture and Curriculum, 28:3*, 226–242

Prodroumou, L. (1992). English as cultural action. *ELT Journal*, 42, 73– 83.

Sandberg, Y. (2017). CLIL in English in Sweden: Why, How and What? Student Perspectives. In C.M. Coonan, L. Favaro & M. Menegale (Eds.), *A Journey through the Content and Language Integrated Learning Landscape: Problems and Prospects*. (pp. 29–44). Newcastle: Cambridge Scholars Publishing.

Sandberg, Y. (2015). CLIL Classroom Interaction Challenges: Translanguaging and Genre as Pedagogic Tools? In C. Gitsaki & T. Alexiou (Eds.), *Current issues in second/foreign language teaching and teacher development : Research and Practice* (pp. 212–227). Newcastle: Cambridge Scholars Publishing.

The future of education and skills. Education 2030. OECD 2018. http://www.oecd.org/education/2030/E2030%20Position%20Paper%20(05.04.2018).pdf. [Access 15 May 2019].

The Worldwide Educating for the Future Index A benchmark for the skills of tomorrow. The Economist Intelligence Unit Limited 2017. https://dkf1ato8y5dsg.cloudfront.net/uploads/5/80/eiu-yidan-prize-educating-for-the-future-wp-final.pdf.

eTwinning webpage, https://etwinning.pl/.

Łukasz Zarzycki

Pedagogical University, Kraków, Poland

The Implementation of YouTube Resources in Language Learning

Abstract: YouTube is now used by over 1.8 billion users every day.[1] This chapter aims at exploring YouTube's resources in order to clarify whether YouTube can play an educational role in language learning. YouTube video clips are becoming more and more popular among English language learners. The author presents numerous language learning resources which can be watched free of charge to practice various language learning skills. The chapter offers a detailed analysis of different YouTube channels which are recommended for effective classroom application. Moreover, the chapter presents ideas on how to implement YouTube resources to improve the learning process of the English language and provides the criteria for assessing YouTube learning clips. Lastly, the author focuses on the pros and cons of implementing YouTube in Computer-Assisted Language Learning (CALL).

Keywords: YouTube, CALL, language learning

1. Introduction

In 2005, YouTube was founded by three former PayPal employees: Chad Hurley, Steve Chen and Jawed Karim (Burgess & Green 2013: 1). Over 2 billion logged-in users visit YouTube each month and every day people watch over a billion hours of video and generate billions of views. More than 70 % of YouTube watch time comes from mobile devices. YouTube has launched local versions in more than 100 countries.[2] The webpage is designed to upload, download and share video clips for both educational and entertaining purposes. Soon after its launching, the webpage started gaining acceptance. The availability of audiovisual content has expanded considerably in the recent decade. The wide variety of materials and their interactive content make YouTube a remarkable tool for learning initiatives. Therefore, language educators and students are encouraged to use YouTube clips for educational purposes. A large number of studies have found that students prefer learning with online resources (see Kumar & Turner

---

1 https://www.businessinsider.com/youtube-user-statistics-2018-5?IR=T

2 https://www.youtube.com/about/press/, *YouTube statistics*, retrieved March 13, 2020.

2006, Jin & Deifell 2013, Stephen & Edwards 2017). However, they frequently need effective methods to identify useful online resources. It is the teacher's duty to make these tools accessible to the students.

There is insufficient literature that reviews the use of YouTube resources in language studying. This chapter aims to propose an informed selection of ideas on how to use YouTube in CALL. Furthermore, the author will review the channels on YouTube concerning English language teaching and provide a short analysis of them. Finally, some possible drawbacks that could be encountered while using online clips will be considered.

2. Review of literature

The connections between YT and the language classroom have been studied from a number of perspectives: the evaluation of YouTube resources (Morain & Swarts 2011; Alhamami, 2013, Tolentino, 2016), categorizing YouTube videos (Berk, 2009; Ghasemi et al. 2011; Hansch et al., 2015), enhancing language skills (Berk, 2009; Watkins and Wilkins, 2011; Buzzetto-More, 2015; Olasina, 2017; Kabooha & Elyas, 2018; Arndt & Woore, 2018), motivation (Oddone, 2011; Klobas et al. 2018), effectiveness (Kelly et al., 2009; Wang and Chen, 2019) and attitudes (Seilstad, 2012, Azurawati et al. 2018). Learning English with the help of YouTube is therefore not a straightforwardly recent phenomenon.

2.1. The types

First, the evaluation of YouTube resources was studied by Morain and Swarts (2011) who presented an approach for evaluating the instructional content of YouTube videos. Their rubric is based on data derived from a comparative study of user-rated YouTube videos. Alhamami (2013) presented a rubric to help teachers select and evaluate the appropriate YouTube language videos for the target audience. Tolentino (2016) conducted the content analysis to examine the content and design quality for videos providing instructional strategies for English language learning teachers on YouTube.

Other studies dealing with the categorization of YouTube videos were made by Berk (2009: 7), who presented a set of video categories which can be implemented in the process of lesson planning. The author distinguished the following types of videos: drama, action, romantic comedy, documentary, TV programs, commercials, college music videos and faculty or student-made videos. Ghasemi et al. (2011) categorized YouTube videos depending on the teacher's instructional language e.g. Is the teacher's instructional language his or her mother tongue or second language? The first type of video, with instruction in teacher's L1, is the one produced by educators who discuss grammar or present a lesson online. The second type is the video produced by native speakers in the form of video blogs. The first types are better for beginners, whereas the second ones are more suitable for more advanced students.

Video clips are implemented in teaching in a number of ways, e.g. as lectures (Filius and Lam, 2009) and video streaming (Swager, 2008). Hansch et al. (2015) presented video types based on the following features:

- Building Rapport
- Virtual field trips
- Manipulating time and space
- Telling stories
- Motivating learners
- Historical footage
- Demonstrations
- Visual juxtaposition
- Multimedia presentation

The figure below shows a comprehensive list of video types which are popular in YouTube learning:

Figure 1: Types of videos in online learning (Hansch et al., 2015: 12).

Hansch et al. (2015: 20) present an overview of "production styles." They add that "it is possible to combine two or more of them in one video." Here is a list of several production styles:

Figure 2: A catalogue of various production styles (Hansch et al. 2015: 21).

In the "production styles" catalogue by Hansch et al. (2015), a list of questions are posed to assist the instructor in determining which "production style" is relevant for the specific teaching lesson. For instance, in the case of "Actual Paper/Whiteboard," they ask: "Can the viewer easily read what is being written?," "Is the content obscured as it is being written?," "What is added by recording physical writing, rather than digital?"

2.2. The use

Watkins and Wilkins (2011) analysed diverse ways of using YouTube by teachers to teach English and to stimulate students. They stress the usefulness of online streaming videos to improve conversation, listening skills, pronunciation, vocabulary, reading comprehension and writing:

> YouTube can be a valuable tool through which multiple foreign language skills can be taught. Using YouTube both inside and outside the classroom can enhance conversation, listening, and pronunciation skills. YouTube videos can also be utilized as realia to stimulate cultural lessons, enhance exposure to World Englishes, and promote authentic vocabulary development. Even reading and writing activities can be structured around YouTube videos. (Watkins and Wilkins, 2011: 113)

Ghasemi et al. (2011) described the advantages of YouTube in language learning in the following passage:

> The real advantage of YouTube – at least from a language learning point of view – is that it offers authentic examples of everyday English used by everyday people. Yes, this is the challenge as well. Students may enjoy watching these clips, but poor sound quality, pronunciation and slang can make these short videos even more difficult to understand. At the same time use of YouTube videos enables teachers to attach the students to the "real life" nature of these videos. By creating context for these short videos students can be helped to explore a world of online English learning possibilities. YouTube videos can be used in an ELT classroom for various teaching: vocabulary, accents, pronunciations, voice modulation. (Ghasemi et al., 2011: 66)

Buzzetto-More (2015: 55) found in her research that YouTube videos "enhance the engagement, depth of understanding, and the overall satisfaction of students." Some recent studies showed positive educational values of YouTube videos for academic writing (Olasina, 2017) as well as for vocabulary learning (Kabooha & Elyas, 2018; Arndt & Woore, 2018).

Furthermore, studies dealing with the category of the affective sphere, and more specifically enhancing students' motivation were conducted by Oddone (2011) who explored the potential benefits of implementing CLIL classes in language learning contexts with the help of technology. She explained the importance of using YouTube clips as it improves the motivation of students. In her paper, she examined the characteristics of videos and offered several constructive ideas on how to use them in the classroom. Klobas et al. (2018) analysed the compulsive use of YouTube by university students. They also examined the influence of compulsive YouTube use on academic motivation. Their studies revealed that entertainment motivation has a stronger effect than information motivation.

Some studies in the category of the effectiveness of YouTube resources have revealed that YouTube videos are effective as a supplement material and cannot replace a lecturer (Kelly et al., 2009). However, Wang and Chen (2019) evaluated EFL university students' self-regulated language learning on YouTube outside of the classroom and found YouTube videos very useful for students. They interviewed twenty students who had experience of watching English-teaching videos in order to explore their perceptions of their self-learning experience. The study revealed that learning English through watching video clips was more engaging, flexible and more interactive than traditional learning at school. However, this approach was considered less successful for learners who wished to improve English for tests. Azurawati et al. (2018) investigated the students' interests and perceptions on the use of YouTube in learning English. Their study revealed that YouTube helped students complete their course assignments and study tasks.

Finally, Seilstad's (2012) research on students' attitudes explored the use of YouTube clips as a new way of teaching English in Morocco. The study emphasized that implementing YouTube videos in the classroom teaching is a fairly easy technique for producing appropriate and accurate teaching content. Data from students' questionnaires contrasted with the final results of students in previous semesters showed the legitimacy and usefulness of using YouTube videos.

In conclusion, the literature reveals that YouTube as an educational tool has been studied from a number of perspectives: the evaluation of YouTube resources, categorizing YouTube videos, enhancing language skills and motivation, exploring the effectiveness and attitudes. However, there is not enough research yet on the specific YouTube resources. Some studies focused on how to assess the YouTube resources but did not provide any feedback in the form of pedagogical recommendations for teachers i.e. teaching channels. This chapter seeks to fill this gap. The proper selection of YouTube teaching channels is essential as clips can have a strong impact on the emotions and success experience of a student. In a learning scenario, language instructors have to determine the result they wish to achieve. After watching videos students may feel relaxed, excited, whimsy, angry or even sleepy. If implemented improperly, videos may distract and minimize students' learning.

3. Criteria for evaluating and choosing YouTube language learning materials.

According to Mackey and Gass (2005: 175) watching clips "allows the researcher to analyse language use in greater depth." In most cases, YouTube videos are uploaded after a lesson has taken place. Therefore, educators are able to evaluate the online material before they show it to the students or before they prepare their own teaching video.

Alhamami (2013) provided several legitimate criteria of evaluating YouTube learning videos or creating new ones. He classified them into five groups:

1. Video characteristics

This group covers technical elements of clips e.g. sound quality, video quality. The sound and video quality has an influence on the content of the lecture. For instance, producing low sound quality of clips can cause misunderstanding – the voice of educators can be difficult to hear. Moreover, the clip should be of appropriate length so as not to distract students. The tags here need to be correlated with the clip under the right category.

2. Attractiveness

Learner should have fun while watching videos. Furthermore, the clip must include items like music in the background, subtitles and pictures. Educator should show enthusiasm about the lesson while teaching online and has an eye contact with students.

3. Clarity

This group concerns questions about teacher's body language, materials and the speed of voice. Effective language educators should try to speak neither quickly nor slowly and should use appropriate body language. The subtitles should not be used in different colours so as not to distract students but some grammatical issues need to be highlighted with various colours using pens, rulers and even signs.

4. Reaction

Teachers should answer students' questions in the comments and delete vulgar comments under YouTube videos. YouTube is a self-study resource and teachers need to react to comments and check how many people liked or disliked the video, how many times the video has been watched.

5. Content

The last group in the assessment process of YouTube videos is content. For instance, teachers should check if the video contains steps such as introduction, main stage and conclusion. It is also essential to avoid unnecessary commercial ads, personal stories in the videos, culturally sensitive materials. The title of the video should reflect the content of the video. The educator needs to define difficult terms or words, repeat important grammar points and summarize the video lesson.

The above criteria for assessing and choosing the appropriate learning content are not the only ones in the field of research. Berk's criteria (2009) are rated from "G" (for general audiences) to "NR" (no restrictions). "G" videos can be used for general audiences with no restrictions, whereas "NR" clips are not allowed to be watched at all since they are extremely vulgar. Berk (2009) continues that:

> More important are the content ratings for graphic violence, obscene language, nudity, sexuality, and gore. Commercial movies and music videos are out of control. Anything and everything are used to attract audiences. If a video clip or the whole movie is going to be used as a teaching tool, criteria must be established for what is appropriate and acceptable in a teaching-learning context. (Berk 2009: 6)

Berk (2009), following his research, proposes a few additional sets of parameters to judge and consider before producing or using a video from YouTube:

1. The students' characteristics (age, grade level, gender, ethnicity, language dominance)
2. The offensiveness of the video (irrelevant content for showing the video: put-downs or ridicule of females, racial and ethnic groups, professions, politicians and celebrities; mental or physical abuse of anyone; drug use.
3. The video structure (length – as short as possible; context – authentic everyday language use; actions/visual cues – action should relate directly to purpose; a limited number of characters – too many can be distracting.

Lastly, YouTube contains a great number of ads. They are frequently displayed every few minutes and can distract students' attention significantly. Some clips are protected by copyright law and are illegally uploaded on YouTube.

4. The analysis of English learning resources and channels on YouTube

4.1. Methodology

Choosing the appropriate keywords is essential in searching for videos on YouTube. Keywords below will support teachers in finding the target clips:

- *Learn English,*
- *English grammar,*
- *Learn English for beginners,*
- *English pronunciation,*
- *English spelling,*
- *How to learn English,*
- *Language learning methods,*
- *Advanced grammar of English,*
- *Language clips,*
- *Language learning music,*
- *English for kids,*
- *Animated learning videos,*
- *Learn English with subtitles.*

The following section concentrates on the analysis of selected video materials available on YouTube according to the criteria put forward in the subject literature and outlined in the previous section.

4.2. The Analysis

The amount of materials, English teaching resources, video clips and YouTube channels is immense. The creators of YouTube English learning videos are school teachers, university lecturers, companies and language product providers. The produced material on YouTube can be either professional and helpful in learning English or amateur and unattractive. An extensive research into informative and stimulating resources consumes a lot of time but certainly is valuable for future lesson planning. YouTube allows to find useful learning resources due to categories such as education (available on www.youtube.com/education). The selection of YouTube channels listed in the following part was made on the basis of Alhamami (2013) and Berk's (2009) criteria for assessing the learning content. In accordance with Alhamami's recommendations, the channels with learning clips include items like music in the background, subtitles and pictures, they are of good sound and video quality. Teachers often use body language in the clips and speak neither slowly nor quickly. Moreover, teachers react to comments below their clips and no vulgar language was found. The YouTube teachers introduce the content of their lessons and summarize it. Finally, the clips offer lessons for all language proficiency levels. If implemented appropriately, the channels below can improve language learning by teaching pronunciation, vocabulary, accents, varieties of English, grammar and improving students' listening comprehension.

4.2.1. The list

The collection below offers the names of professional YouTube channels with the links and information on the content of the channel. It testifies to the variety of topics and instructional modes used.

A. Spoken language.

Figure 3. YouTube channel: *Speak English with Mr Duncan.*

Webpage address:
https://www.youtube.com/channel/UC8pPDhxSn1nee70LRKJ0p3g
Content: lessons on various topics such as fashion, slang, news. The emphasis is put on spoken English.

Figure 4. YouTube channel: *VOA Learning English.*

Webpage address:
https://www.youtube.com/channel/UCKyTokYo0nK2OA-az-sDijA
Content: the channel offers subtitled news reports which are read at slower speeds.

Figure 5. YouTube channel: *Learn American English.*

Webpage address:
https://www.youtube.com/user/learnenglish232?feature=watch
Content: common American spoken slang, idioms, phrasal verbs.

Figure 6. YouTube channel: *Rachel's English.*

Webpage address: https://www.youtube.com/user/rachelsenglish
Content: learn English with TV, learn English with movies, American accent, pronunciation, American English vs British English, intonation.

Figure 7. YouTube channel: *Learn English with Let's Talk – Free English Lessons.*

Webpage address:
https://www.youtube.com/user/learnexmumbai
Content: tips to improve English speaking, English grammar lessons, spoken English lessons, English phrases and expressions, accent training, idioms.

B. Integrating external information such as culture.

Figure 8. YouTube channel: *Learn English with EnglishClass101.com.*

Webpage address:
https://www.youtube.com/channel/UCeTVoczn9NOZA9blls3YgUg
Content: covers aspects of American and British culture.

C. For beginners and young learners.

Figure 9. YouTube channel: *Real English.*

Webpage address:
https://www.youtube.com/channel/UCUqbE6Sd6DW6M6ZBkZFDfmA
Content: recommended for beginners, videos with subtitles and exercises.

Figure 10. YouTube channel: *BBC Learning English.*

Webpage address:
https://www.youtube.com/channel/UCHaHD477h-FeBbVh9Sh7syA
Content: free English language lessons, real-life situations, interviews, cartoons.

Figure 11. YouTube channel: *British Council: Learn English Kids.*

Webpage address:
https://www.youtube.com/channel/UC-qWJlvaPME3MWvrY-yjXeA
Content: songs, nursery rhymes, animated videos and cartoons with subtitles in English. The channel helps kids to improve memory, study new verbs and expressions.

Figure 12. YouTube channel: *JenniferESL*

Webpage address:
https://www.youtube.com/channel/UCEKXieT70wByfvZwP1CxdPQ
Content: lessons for beginners, lessons to improve your writing in English, lessons on grammar with special focus on pronunciation.

D. English for Specific Purposes.

Figure 13. YouTube channel: *Business English Pod.*

Webpage address:
https://www.youtube.com/channel/UCIiFsAO2Gh_vu8OStpjl16A
Content: lessons on topics such as supply chain management, finance/economics and contract law.

Webpage address: https://www.youtube.com/user/Linguaspectrum
Content: lessons about the vocabulary which students need at an airport, about insects or types of musical instruments, lessons on grammar, spelling.

Figure 14. YouTube channel: *Britlish- Learn British English.*

E. Improving all skills.

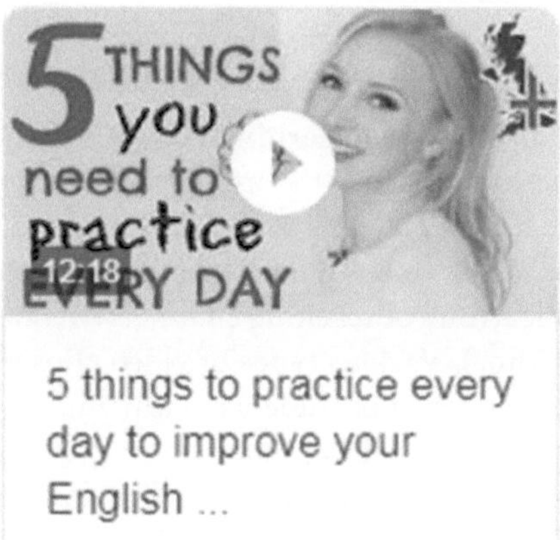

Figure 15. YouTube channel: *English with Lucy.*

Webpage address:
https://www.youtube.com/channel/UCz4tgANd4yy8Oe0iXCdSWfA
Content: English speaking skills, British English Pronunciation, vocabulary, English Grammar, study techniques, British Expressions, Business English, interviews, vlogs, English listening practice.

4.2.2. Pedagogical concerns

The implementation of teaching or learning clips poses several questions, among them the following:

1. What cognitive techniques do we want to improve?
2. Do we want students to learn with authentic videos or adapted ones?
3. Should we watch very long YouTube videos in the classroom?
4. How about subtitles? Should we use them or not?
5. Is a video appropriate for students' age and the level of language?

All the aforementioned questions should be considered before implementing videos. They relate specifically to the evaluation criteria according to which the list above was compiled. The list demonstrates directly that in the classroom teaching, there are various applications of videos: improving listening, interpreting graphical clues in order to facilitate comprehension. Photos can be used to start a debate or a reflection in groups.

Educators play a vital role since they are accountable for providing an adequate learning environment. They need to evaluate and choose video clips which are suitable for use in the classrooms. Furthermore, teachers have to set exercises and assignments that promote students' participation and cooperation.

5. Conclusions and pedagogical recommendations

The success of YouTube clips as a learning resource can differ depending on the quality of instruction and it is the assessment of YouTube videos which allows to enhance the benefits of clips used for educational purposes. The brisk expansion in the number of videos uploaded and the quality of clips has led to endless popularity of learning or teaching channels (frequently with more than a million hits on YouTube). Various types of video clips available on YouTube are a result of the strong interest of students in learning English using YouTube resources and subscribing to teaching channels.

Teachers must be very selective when using clips during their lessons if they want to enhance students' learning skills. Therefore, videos chosen by language instructors need to be evaluated based on several factors (e.g. video characteristics, attractiveness, clarity, reaction, content) clarified previously in this chapter. There are some clear advantages for the learners to study English from YouTube clips e.g. watching videos at any time at home, editing videos (pausing and skipping) or repeating the clips several times. YouTube provides examples of real English used in daily life and can be implemented by the language instructor to teach pronunciation, vocabulary, accents, varieties of English, grammar and improve students' listening comprehension. This can also be an assignment or task for students to find the right materials. It is also possible to replace the word "English" with any other word in your target language to find the right learning materials. YouTube provides the option to open your own account. It will help teachers or students subscribe to your favourite learning channels. Including the evaluation of the video materials in your lessons will help students be aware of the quality and efficacy of videos.

However, it is necessary to note that certain drawbacks of YouTube teaching videos do exist. To begin with, numerous videos are protected by copyright law and are uploaded illegally. Furthermore, despite the vast amount of learning resource on YouTube, some teacher instruction and support in selecting the appropriate video clips for the learners can be required so as to avoid wasting time on searching for useful resources. Albeit, YouTube blocks vulgar or perverse material, some topics of lessons or language might be offensive. Instructors of young students should be aware of such content and take it into consideration while selecting materials. The author's review of English learning resources and channels on YouTube offers a selection of non-vulgar and inoffensive learning and teaching materials recommended to implement in the teaching process.

References

Alhamami, M. (2013). Observation of YouTube Language Learning Videos (YouTube LLVS). *Teaching English with Technology, 13*(3), 3–17.

Arndt, H.L. & Woore, R. (2018). Vocabulary learning from watching YouTube videos and reading blog posts. *Language Learning & Technology, 22*(3), 124–142.

Azurawati, Z., Farahidatul, A., Rafidah, A., Nurul, F., Muhd, S., & Nooraileen, I. (2018). University Students' Perceptions of YouTube Usage in ESL Classrooms. *International Journal of Academic Research in Business and Social Sciences, 8*(1), 541–553.

Berk, R. (2009). Multimedia teaching with video clips: TV, movies, YouTube, and mtvU in the college classroom. *International Journal of Technology in Teaching and Learning, 5*(1), 1–21.

Burgess, J. & Green, J. (2013). *YouTube: Online Video and Participatory Culture.* Chicago: John Wiley & Sons.

Buzzetto-More, N. (2015). Student Attitudes Towards the Integration of YouTube in Online, Hybrid, and Web-Assisted Courses: An Examination of the Impact of Course Modality on Perception. *MERLOT Journal of Online Learning and Teaching*, 11(1), 55–73.

Filius, R., & Lam, I. (2009). *Rapport evaluatie weblectures Universiteit Utrecht*. Utrecht.

Ghasemi, B., Hashemi, M., & Bardine, S.H. (2011). Utube and language learning. *Procedia – Social and Behavioral Sciences, 28*, 63–67.

Hansch, A., Hillers, L., McConachie, K. & Newman, C. (2015). Video and Online Learning: Critical Reflections and Findings from the Field. *HIIG Discussion Paper Series*. Alexander von Humboldt Institute für Internet und Gesellschaft. Retrieved from https://ssrn.com/abstract=2577882

Jin, L. & Deifell, E. (2013*)*. Foreign Language Learners' Use and Perception of Online Dictionaries: A Survey Study. *MERLOT Journal of Online Learning and Teaching, 9*(4), 515–533.

Kabooha, R. & Elyas, T. (2018). The Effects of YouTube in Multimedia Instruction for Vocabulary Learning: Perceptions of EFL Students and Teachers. *English Language Teaching, 11*(2), 72–81.

Kelly, M., McGrath, M., & Cannon, G. (2009). A multi-method study to determine the effectiveness of, and student attitudes to, online instructional videos for teaching clinical nursing skills. *Nurse Education Today, 29*(3), 292–300.

Klobas, J., McGill, T., Moghavvemi, S., & Paramanathan, T. (2018). Compulsive YouTube usage: A comparison of use motivation and personality effects. *Computers in Human Behavior, 87*, 129–139.

Kumar, D. & Turner, J. (2006). Education for the 21st Century – Impact of ICT and Digital Resources: IFIP 19th World Computer Congress. *TC-3 Education*. Santiago, Chile: Springer.

Mackey, A., & Gass, S. (2005). *Second Language Research: Methodology and Design*. Mahwah NJ: Lawrence Erlbaum.

Morain, M., & Swarts, J. (2011). YouTutorial: A Framework for Assessing Instructional Online Video. *Technical Communication Quarterly, 21*(1), 6–24.

Oddone, C. (2011). Using Videos from YouTube and Websites in CLIL Classroom. *Studies About Languages, 18*, 105–110.

Olasina, G. (2017). An evaluation of educational values of YouTube videos for academic writing. *The African Journal of Information Systems, 9*(4), 231–261.

Prensky, M. (2009). Make Those You Tubes! *Educational Technology*, 1–4.

Seilstad, B. (2012). Using tailor-made YouTube videos as a preteaching strategy for English language learners in Morocco: Towards a hybrid language learning course. *Teaching English with Technology, 4*, 31–47.

Stephen, C. & Edwards, S. (2017). *Young Children Playing and Learning in a Digital Age: A Cultural and Critical Perspective*. London: Routledge.

Swager, P. (2008). Nieuwe technologie. *Develop*, *4*, 90–94. Retrieved from http://www.corporateeducation.com/files/Develop_2008-4.pdf

Tolentino, C. (2016). *Content Analysis of TeacherTube and YouTube Videos for Instructing English Language Learners*. Honolulu: University of Hawaii at Manoa.

Wang, H. & Chen C.W. (2019). Learning English from YouTubers: English L2 learners' self-regulated language learning on YouTube. *Innovation in Language Learning and Teaching*. Retrieved from https://www.tandfonline.com/doi/abs/10.1080/17501229.2019.1607356?needAccess=true&journalCode=rill20

Watkins, J. & Wilkins, M. (2011). Using YouTube in EFL Classroom. *Language Education in Asia*, *2*(1), 113–119.

Online sources

1. https://www.businessinsider.com/youtube-user-statistics-2018-5?IR=T
2. https://www.youtube.com/about/press/, *YouTube statistics*,
3. https://www.youtube.com/channel/UC8pPDhxSn1nee70LRKJ0p3g
4. https://www.youtube.com/channel/UCeTVoczn9NOZA9blls3YgUg
5. https://www.youtube.com/channel/UCUqbE6Sd6DW6M6ZBkZFDfmA
6. https://www.youtube.com/channel/UCHaHD477h-FeBbVh9Sh7syA
7. https://www.youtube.com/channel/UC-qWJlvaPME3MWvrY-yjXeA
8. https://www.youtube.com/channel/UCIiFsAO2Gh_vu8OStpjl16A
9. https://www.youtube.com/channel/UCKyTokYo0nK2OA-az-sDijA
10. https://www.youtube.com/channel/UCEKXieT70wByfvZwP1CxdPQ
11. https://www.youtube.com/user/Linguaspectrum
12. https://www.youtube.com/user/learnenglish232?feature=watch
13. https://www.youtube.com/channel/UCz4tgANd4yy8Oe0iXCdSWfA
14. https://www.youtube.com/user/rachelsenglish
15. https://www.youtube.com/user/learnexmumbai

Studies in Computer Assisted Language Learning

Edited by Anna Turula

Vol. 1 Anna Turula / Maria Chojnacka (eds.): CALL for Bridges between School and Academia. 2015.

Vol. 2 Mariusz Marczak / Jarosław Krajka (eds.): CALL for Openness. 2016.

Vol. 3 Joanna Pitura / Shannon Sauro (eds.): CALL for Mobility. 2018.

Vol. 4 Anna Turula / Anita Buczek-Zawiła (eds.): CALL for Background. 2021.

www.peterlang.com

www.ingramcontent.com/pod-product-compliance
Ingram Content Group UK Ltd.
Pitfield, Milton Keynes, MK11 3LW, UK
UKHW041829100926
8556IPUK00002B/81

9 783631 845295